Theory for Theatre Studies: Space

Online resources to accompany this book are available at https://bloomsbury.com/uk/theory-for-theatre-studies-space-9781350006072. Please type the URL into your web browser and follow the instructions to access the Companion Website. If you experience any problems, please contact Bloomsbury at: contact@bloomsbury.com

Theory for Theatre Studies meets the need for accessible, mid-length volumes that unpack keywords that lie at the core of the discipline. Aimed primarily at undergraduate students and secondarily at postgraduates and researchers, volumes feature both background material historicizing the term and original, forward-looking research into intersecting theoretical trends in the field. Case studies ground volumes in praxis, and additional resources online ensure readers are equipped with the necessary skills and understanding as they move deeper into the discipline.

Series editors:

Susan Bennett, University of Calgary, Canada
Kim Solga, Western University, Canada

Theory for Theatre Studies: Space,
Kim Solga

Forthcoming titles

Theory for Theatre Studies: Sound, Susan Bennett
Theory for Theatre Studies: Movement, Rachel Fensham
Theory for Theatre Studies: Emotion, Peta Tait
Theory for Theatre Studies: Economics, Michael McKinnie
Theory for Theatre Studies: Memory, Milija Gluhovic

Theory for Theatre Studies: Space

Kim Solga

Series editors:
Susan Bennett and Kim Solga

methuen | drama
LONDON • NEW YORK • OXFORD • NEW DELHI • SYDNEY

METHUEN DRAMA
Bloomsbury Publishing Plc
50 Bedford Square, London, WC1B 3DP, UK
1385 Broadway, New York, NY 10018, USA

BLOOMSBURY, METHUEN DRAMA and the Methuen Drama logo are trademarks of Bloomsbury Publishing Plc

First published in Great Britain 2019

For legal purposes the Acknowledgments on p. ix constitute an extension of this copyright page.

Series design by Louise Dugdale
Cover image © Henrik Sorensen / Getty images

A catalogue record for this book is available from the British Library.

A catalog record for this book is available from the Library of Congress.

ISBN: HB: 978-1-350-00607-2
PB: 978-1-350-00606-5
ePDF: 978-1-350-00609-6
eBook: 978-1-350-00608-9

Series: Theory for Theatre Studies

Typeset by Integra Software Services Pvt. Ltd.
Printed and bound in India

To find out more about our authors and books visit www.bloomsbury.com and sign up for our newsletters.

For all of my dear friends
at Queen Mary, University of London

CONTENTS

ACKNOWLEDGMENTS

I owe my principal and most heartfelt thanks to Susan Bennett, my series co-editor, for inviting me to join the *Theory for Theatre Studies* project and for working closely with me on the development of this volume. Although Susan has been a mentor, friend, and role model to me for many years now, this is the first time we have collaborated so fulsomely on an academic project. It is a true pleasure to learn from such a respectful, forthright, generous, and professional scholar.

Thanks to Mark Dudgeon and everyone at Bloomsbury, including Susan Furber and Lara Bateman: for encouraging the development of this series, championing it through its long initial gestation, and supporting our vision for a robust list of innovative but accessible books that can address the needs of students and researchers alike.

Thanks to Western University for the sabbatical leave on which I wrote this text, and for research support in both the initial and final stages of its preparation. I'm particularly grateful to my research assistants, Selena Huband and Jaclyn Reed, for help with manuscript prep.

Thanks to Dylan Robinson for sharing work in progress with me as I worked on the final parts of this book; his eloquent writing serves as the inspiration for much of what appears in Section Three.

Finally, thanks to Karen for asking: "have you started the book yet?" And to Dhurin for asking: "is the book finished yet?" (And also for the celebratory biryani, when at last the answer was: YES.)

SERIES PREFACE

Theory for Theatre Studies (TfTS) is a series of introductory theoretical monographs intended for both undergraduate and postgraduate students as well as researchers branching out into fresh fields. It aims to introduce constellations of ideas, methods, theories, and rubrics central to the working concerns of scholars in theatre and performance studies at the opening of the twenty-first century. With a primary focus on twentieth-century developments, TfTS volumes offer accessible and provocative engagements with critical theory that inspire new ways of thinking theory in important disciplinary and interdisciplinary modes.

The series features full-length volumes explicitly aimed at unpacking sets of ideas that have coalesced around carefully chosen key terms in theatre and performance, such as space, sound, bodies, memory, movement, economies, and emotion. TfTS volumes do not aggregate existing essays, but rather provide a careful, fresh synthesis of what extensive reading by our authors reveals to be key nodes of interconnection between related theoretical models. The goal of these texts is to introduce readers to a wide variety of critical approaches and to unpack the complex theory useful for both performance analysis and creation.

Each volume in the series focuses on one specific set of theoretical concerns, constellated around a term that has become central to understanding the social and political labour of theatre and performance work at the turn of the millennium. The organization of each book follows a common template: Section One includes a historical overview of interconnected theoretical models, Section Two features extended case studies using twentieth- and twenty-first-century performances, and

Section Three looks ahead, as our authors explore important new developments in their constellation. Each volume is broad enough in scope to look laterally across its topic for compelling connections to related concerns, yet specific enough to be comprehensive in its assessment of its particular term. The ideas explored and explained through lively and detailed case studies provide diverse critical approaches for reading all kinds of plays and performances as well as starting points for practical exploration.

Each book includes a further reading section, and features a companion website with chapter summaries, questions for discussion, and a host of video and other web links.

Susan Bennett (University of Calgary, Canada)
and Kim Solga (Western University, Canada)

Introduction: Making Room for Space at the Theatre

Locate Yourself

This book takes as its subject what came to be known, in the last decade of the twentieth century and the first decade of the twenty-first, as the "spatial turn" in theatre and performance studies. This turn—a shift toward a new subject as a focus of theory and criticism—made issues of space and place[1] central to the investigation of meaning-making at the theatre, in acts of staged or curated performance outside traditional theatre spaces, and in performances of "everyday life" (the central critical object for the discipline of performance studies). This turn involved the development of theoretical frameworks for thinking about how space, as an independent but also an *interdependent* function of theatrical composition (along with, for example, acting bodies, an audience, and a script, whether pre-conceived or devised), generates aesthetic, social, and political value for producers and consumers of the performance event. Thinking carefully, and systematically, about space's place at the theatre also, ultimately, provoked a deliberate *recognition of the politics of space*—or, more precisely, of the way politics *takes place*, operates as a function of space and place, in the theatre and in the world. The examination of the politics of space in and through the theatre, I will argue throughout this book, is central to the way space is recognized and deployed as both a theatrical and a performance property now.

Why politics? How can "space"—one of the simultaneously most boundless and abstract, *and* most grounded and concrete, concepts in the human imaginary—be itself political, or activate the political elsewhere? Space organizes our social relationships; it structures our relations of power (economic, political, gendered, and more). Space may seem kind of obvious, ignorable, a given—space is "just there," after all, all the time—and yet it is the physical, psychical, and social framework that contains and enables all human interaction, as well as all interaction between and among humans and nonhuman inhabitants of the planet. Consider the statement I just made: *that space is arguably one of the simultaneously most boundless and abstract, and most grounded and concrete, concepts in the human imaginary*. It constantly implicates and locates us, and yet it often remains consciously, critically, beyond our grasp (Tompkins 2014: 7; Casey 1997: ix). This paradox is one reason space makes such a fruitful topic for critical discussion, and yet is often hard to talk about, and even harder to talk about *precisely* (see Tompkins 2014). Further, space's epistemological duality—its imaginary potential, coupled with its literal and constant *material* impact on our lives—inevitably transforms it into *territory*, into something to be argued over, fought for, colonized, decolonized, hunted, owned, and lost.

When I say "space," what comes first to your mind? I think immediately about outer space: the world beyond our world, a place I can only grasp in my imagination. In order to make that leap, I think about some of the specific frameworks people in my culture (Anglophone, North American) use to access the concept we call "outer space": the famous telecast of the moon landing in 1969; the "the final frontier" of the *Star Trek* franchise; the physical tools our culture has built for launching and flying vehicles toward Mars, Jupiter, and beyond our galaxy. Notice that these touch points—film and TV images, brand catch-phrases, technical inventions—are all products of human imagination. They represent some of the ways we have collectively sought to make "outer space" our own: to tame it, conquer it, transform it into something we can hold and control. Indeed, "outer space" has been historically, particularly during the "Cold War" in the middle of the twentieth century, a site for international competition; in the 1960s the United States and the former USSR raced to beat one another to the moon, aiming to use that achievement as evidence of their mastery of the other on earth. During the Cold War, "outer space" was the ground upon which *realpolitik* between nations on earth played out.

When I think about outer space, though, I don't just think of film stills and geopolitics. I also remember how miniscule our galaxy is, relative to the vastness aerospace science tells us is our universe. I think about how "outer space" is an English-language term invented to contain what is literally not containable: the possibility that the broader spatial field in which the creatures alive on earth exist has no outer limit and that "space" is, in material fact, unimaginable endlessness.

I find that thought terrorizing; it drives me immediately inward, into the hold-able, knowable world of my room. *My place*. And here, again, we can find—counterintuitively, perhaps—the latent political potential of "space" as a container of human agency. Think about what your room means to you. My room (the room in my house in which I write and read and research) is filled with items that articulate the person I identify as "me"; these items, carefully placed around my space, give me the props, the tools I require in order to perform, for myself, a clear, bounded, grounded sense of who I am and can be. (As Vesela Kucheva delightfully argues, our homes are scenographies built for the performances we continuously, simultaneously enact and observe within them [2013: 1–2].)

Here, I might remind us that subjectivity is not inherent; I was not born "Kim." I became (in fact, continue becoming) the Kim

I am, thanks to a combination of things. First, intersubjective articulation (spoken aloud, but also unconsciously communicated) among family, friends, teachers, and other acquaintances (what twentieth-century theorists like Jacques Derrida and Jacques Lacan, associated with the poststructuralist movement, would call part of my immediate discursive field). Second, interactions with social and political structures specific to my national and cultural contexts (what Michel Foucault or Pierre Bourdieu, also post-structural thinkers, would call the Law that hails and surveils us, the surrounds that shape our *habitus*). Third, phenomenal (i.e., felt, touched, perceived) encounters with my immediate worlds, including the world of my childhood home, of my later, adult homes, and of my classrooms, among other places. Influential spatial theorist Gaston Bachelard, as well as phenomenologists like Maurice Merleau-Ponty, would argue that it is not simply the fields of discourse, but also the lived, experiential, material world, and our physical and emotional interactions with that world, that shape subjective coming-into-being. Fourth, the imagined projections (psychical, but also creative) enabled by conscious and unconscious combinations of all of the above encounters. Notice that all of the subjectivating experiences I just listed take place *in space*; they do not simply occupy space (although of course they do that), but they literally em-place me, locate me, root me in a variety of concrete, remembered places even as I move around the world. To the extent my subjecthood obtains, it is performed *in and also through space*, over and over again, by me alongside a rotating host of other actors. And, to the extent my subjecthood is *contested*—or any identity, be it cultural, national, gendered, sexual, social, or racial, is contested—that contest, between various stakeholders, obtains in space, and uses space (just as I use my room filled with treasured objects; just as the Cold War superpowers used "outer space") to reflect each party in the contest as its ideal self, its best self, the self it is continually striving to present to the world.

If this is feeling a bit fuzzy, it might help for us to take a trip to the theatre. Imagine that we are at the Young Vic, a mid-sized, socially conscious, politically left-leaning venue on the South Bank in London, England. It is summer 2012, and we are seeing *A Doll's House*, by Henrik Ibsen, in a contemporary version by British playwright Simon Stephens, directed by Carrie Cracknell. Hattie Morahan plays Nora Helmer, the woman whose middle-class aspirations drive her, by play's end, to an extraordinary discovery about the gendered limits of her world, a discovery that propels her out of her family's home (and into what she might well call "outer space") in order to locate a more expansive sense of her place beyond that small world. Dominic Rowan plays her husband Torvald, a man so comfortable in his identity that he is unable to conceive of anyone wanting to leave his household, ever. (Not that he doesn't seek to control their access to that household, of course; his sense of control over the space of Nora's home grounds *him* in that world quite nicely.) In the scene in which Morahan's Nora confronts Rowan's Torvald, in the final fifteen minutes of the production, both actors enter Nora's small room, one of the smallest spaces (the other is, instructively, Torvald's study) on the rotating set that represents their small apartment.

(This production is available to stream on Digital Theatre Plus; I recommend watching the final scene before reading further, if you have access.)

In her room, Nora is at first measured in her insistence that she must leave Torvald and her children; when her arguments do not land (Torvald is somewhat drunk, as well as obstinate in his role as the benevolent patriarch), she begins to yell, to cry, to use her body unexpectedly (hitting Torvald, for example) in an attempt to break free of the room, of her wifehood, of her sense of entrapment in the household and the social role it dictates to her. Finally, Torvald reminds her that she is above all a wife and mother; Nora then shouts, emphatically through tears, that she is above all a human being. She gathers her bag and her coat, walks out of the small bedroom into the hallway, and leaves the apartment, exiting the set and departing up the staircase stage right—into unknown space.

We can learn a huge amount about the politics of space and place at (and beyond) the theatre from Ibsen's taut interpersonal drama. Nora's sense of self is performed, for her and for us and for Torvald, over the course of both the play and this particular performance of it in relation to objects in her space—her Christmas tree, the presents she has bought for her children, her decoration of the house for the holiday, her contraband stash of sweets, her Tarantella costume, and (of course) the mailbox that contains the incriminating letter from Krogstad, the letter that will reveal her criminal action to her husband and place her marriage in jeopardy. Our sense of Nora (and her sense of herself) emerges primarily from her interactions *with things in space*, as she moves toward and away from and around them. (Morahan emphasizes this powerfully as she fidgets with items, her hands constantly busy with things or flying at her face and temples when not, as though she is desperate always to be somewhere, or busy with something, else.[2]) Torvald's sense of self is similarly produced by stuff: he is every inch the product of his private study, where he spends the bulk of his time with his back to the audience and his door closed to his wife. He retreats almost immediately to his study each time he returns home, and when visitors arrive to speak to him they are shown into the study—he doesn't come out to meet them. Torvald's security of person, and of power, emerges from his groundedness in this tiny, particular, well-patrolled place, just as Nora's deracination is visible in her fidgeting discomfort with the objects and visitors she fawns over a bit too much throughout the play. Torvald inhabits the spaces of the set, of his home, with firm, settled conviction; Nora, by contrast, seems slightly uncomfortable in every room.

These actor-object relations come to a head in the final scene, as Nora exits stage right. Their conflict is both personal and political (and was even more so in Ibsen's own, proto-feminist moment in history): Nora seeks to become more human woman than wife-child and mother-child to Torvald and their babies, while Torvald, wielding the power he holds as a nineteenth-century, middle-class man over his home and family, fails to grasp Nora's pleas because he is unable, physically but also imaginatively, to inhabit the places to which she has been relegated. Their home is a public, social space as well as a private place, an imagined space as well as a literal one; Nora's longings (a lovely Christmas; nice things for the home in the new year), however creative she has been with Torvald's money, cannot quite make up for the fact that Torvald's power, as holder of the pocketbook and the mailbox keys, determines the limits of her access, her ability to make her spatial imaginings take material shape. Their final argument resonates as a profoundly political exploration of the gendered power imbalance many of us continue to live with, at work and at home, nearly 140 years after the play was written. This is precisely because resources—not the least of which is access to and influence over space—remain unequally distributed in many parts of the globe according to gender, sexuality, class, race, ability, and ethnicity.

The politics of this particular scene, this particular play, are not restricted to the stage and set, however. Notice that, in the commentary above, I've been concerned with two particular aspects of theatrical space: (1) the fictional world of the play, originally conceived by Ibsen, and the ways that world takes shape through interactions among his characters and between characters and the objects he prescribes for the setting; and (2) the production's scenography, the ways in which Cracknell's designer (Ian MacNeil) here interprets Ibsen's stage directions and textual cues in conjunction with the rest of the creative team. There are at least two other aspects of theatrical space that should concern us, however: (3) the spaces inside the theatre building that are not on the stage (which might include auditorium space, lobby space, office spaces for theatre workers, and backstage spaces where carpenters, set builders, stage managers, and the rest of the offstage crew accomplish their labor); and (4) the spaces beyond the theatre building that place *this* building, and the work it showcases, in its local, regional, national, and international public spheres.

The Young Vic styles itself as a social hub. Built on the border between two of London's poorest boroughs (Lambeth and Southwark), it actively serves those who live in its immediate community with a privately funded free ticket scheme, internships, and neighborhood-focused workshops and community shows. In this respect, its leadership might argue that the Young Vic has been conceived as a space of access for those typically restricted economically or socially in their movements around London, an incredibly expensive global city. At the same time, though, the Young Vic draws a fairly well-heeled, middle class, broadly liberal audience keen to see socially minded theatre in a popular entertainment district (London's South Bank) where they can also have a nice dinner or enjoy a comfortable drink in the open-plan lobby-bar. These audience members—of which I must count myself one—might well have cheered Morahan's sharp parting words in Cracknell's production, as those words affirmed their senses of self and world; while an extraordinary leap into the physical and emotional unknown of "outer space" for Nora, her exit may have been profoundly self-grounding for many of those already-liberal, already-feminist subjects watching her. They certainly were for me: the production confirmed for me a sense of feeling "at home" at the Young Vic (Solga and Tompkins 2017), as it cemented the political values I share with the theatre (feminist, community-oriented, social justice-oriented). For others, however—especially those local visitors who may have taken advantage of the theatre's free ticket scheme for the first time, having never seen this play, or maybe even *any* play, on stage before—Nora's departure could easily have resonated as an opening-up, a reflection on what it might take to reach into a new world, to break out of social or spatial traps that feel all too familiar. This is something the Young Vic's free ticket scheme—part of the "it's a big world in here" marketing campaign (Solga and Tompkins 2017)—is expressly designed to encourage and affirm.

The Way Ahead

My brief analysis of Cracknell's production of *A Doll's House* reveals how complex the interactions among theatre's multiple spatial layers may be for artists, audiences, and critics. The contours of a fictional script may be transparently supported, or productively challenged, by the set and lighting designs created to stage that script. Meanings created inside the play-world by scenographers, actors, directors, and lighting designers may resonate with, or chafe against, messages generated as part of a theatre's attempts to locate itself within (or even beyond) its community for marketing and development purposes. Those meanings may also intersect with debates about public versus private spaces, and access to or ownership of those spaces, under discussion in the larger social worlds in which the theatre is located—debates that may in turn enable productive critical commentary about how theatre companies and venues, playwrights and directors, and other cultural stakeholders spend their social capital, or seek to obtain more of it. The spaces of the theatre, in other words, are fictional and physical, economic and artistic, creative and quotidian, internal and external; they are woven intricately together, and they are deeply embedded in theatre's inherent political potential as a public, social, and interactive art form. It's worth bearing in mind, as we move forward, that the place at which Western theatre locates its origin story is a public auditorium in ancient Greece, a venue expressly designed to share socially topical stories and encourage thoughtful discussion about them in the service of maintaining a robust democracy.

So: how do we get from this starting point—theatre's spaces are layered and complex; theatre's spaces operate politically—to the kind of analysis I just demonstrated? What are the theoretical tools that scholars use to talk in a thorough and precise way about theatrical space? How and where do these tools intersect, and what can their intersection teach us? What do we learn, for example, when an economic approach, or an architectural approach, is used to understand the different ways theatre venues operate in the urban ecology of a global city (Carlson 1989; McKinnie 2007)? When a formalist approach is used to make sense of the relationship between spectator and spectacle in site-specific performance (Schechner

1973)? When a *feminist* approach is added to help make sense of the same (Levin 2014)?

Much scholarship about space and place at the theatre is broadly semiotic, which means it reads space as one of several theatrical languages, or sign systems, at play in performance. (For a traditional, but helpfully clear, example of semiotic theatre analysis, see Fischer-Lichte 1992.) Often, scholars writing about theatrical space in this way divide their field of inquiry into categories, representing stage (performance), auditorium (viewing), and lobby/office/workshop (labor) spaces respectively; most follow, to some extent, Gay McAuley's influential taxonomy in her 1999 book *Space in Performance: Making Meaning in the Theatre* (25). For example, Morash and Richards (2013) talk variously about theatre's conceptual, mimetic, and signifying spaces. Tompkins distinguishes among constructed, abstracted, and heterotopic spaces (2014: 1, 27). Fischer-Lichte and Whistutz (2012) organize their edited volume, *Performance and the Politics of Space*, using the headings "Placements and Boundaries"; "Utopia and Heterotopias"; and "Strategies of Spatial Appropriation"—creative wording for a similar semiotic division of meaning.

Space's abstract discursive nature (what I called above the difficulty of speaking about it *precisely*) has invited multiple forms of categorization from theorists interested in examining space as a structure of signification inside or outside of any given theatre building or organization; this methodology offers researchers an effective way to ground space's abstractions in the concrete and particular. Categorizing space before analyzing it is useful because categories orient us; they make their objects fully graspable and useable. However, for this reason they also operate politically. Categories of theatrical space *make* that space appear to us in certain ways, producing "theatrical space" as a series of concrete images in readers' minds. (Consider briefly the distinctions among stage, auditorium, and extra-theatrical work spaces I mentioned a moment ago; when you read that list of classifications, what *actual* places or images came to mind?)

Many theorists of theatrical space trace their roots to groundbreaking writing by Henri Lefebvre, a twentieth-century sociologist[3] and ardent Marxist who first articulated space as socially "produced" rather than given. In *The Production of Space*, Lefebvre argues that space is an effect of (rather than simply a container for) social and political interactions, which in turn means it has enormous impact on the workings of power on human bodies (1991: 26). Primarily semiotic approaches to theatrical space tend to classify and categorize in order carefully to unpick the various, usually interlocking ways in which space is produced (and thus politicized) inside a discrete theatrical event. Cultural materialist approaches to reading theatrical space, meanwhile, often foreground in their analyses the extra-theatrical social and economic contexts in which theatre and performance events take place, paying special attention to the ways those contexts produce the material conditions in which a given theatre building or company is found, and the impact such conditions may in turn have on audience expectation and reaction, funding, and programming. These complementary forms of analysis work very well together, painting a broad but fulsome picture of a theatrical event's complete relationship to space and place, both inside and outside its narrative world.

The theatre, as scenographer and scholar Arnold Aronson writes, is fundamentally "an art of time and space" (2013: 84): those whose design work *literally* shapes the worlds an ordinary stage may become understand well the power of constructed space to define human action, enabling some kinds of becoming while restricting others. Contemporary trends in scenography and design theory mediate between the science-side model of semiotic analysis and the phenomenological and materialist analyses of space that mid-century philosophers like Lefebvre, Henri Bergson, and Gaston Bachelard heralded for theatre's spatial turn. As Sodja Lotker and Richard Gough note: "We move through many scenographies during the day; we go from one environment to another—from actual to virtual, from private to public, from staged to unstaged, from known to unknown. We perform scenographies and they perform us" (2013: 3). Space is constructed by human actions, to be sure—in particular at the theatre!—but once in situ, space also *plays us*. On stage, it makes certain kinds of performances physically and emotionally possible (and renders others potentially impossible, depending on the strategic placement of props or the exigencies of period costumes, for example). Elsewhere, space covertly organizes our working and leisure lives, frames our relationships, and even determines who we see and who remains invisible in plain sight, erased by the limiting perspective that orients our eyes. (This is something we will explore extensively in my third case study in Section Two.) Lotker and Gough, taking the measure of an "expanded" scenography within the context of the twenty-first-century spatial turn (2013: 3), argue that it is no longer possible to view scenography as just "setting" (if it ever was). Nor can we any longer view the work of designers as purely plastic art. Scenography must today be understood as "a body," a disciplinary system with its own rules and logic, one that includes built but also found space, environments that act for and with us even as we re-frame them for our artistic ends. (We will return to this idea at the end of Section One.) Scenography is the *space* in which performance takes place, but it is also the *place* that performs as our ever-present collaborator—and must be reckoned with as such (see also Levin 2009).

Notably, this argument dovetails Lotker and Gough's "expanded" scenography with a host of other ways we might talk about space in performance; the articles collected in their 2013 special issue of *Performance Research* on scenography, for example, touch on urban performance studies, phenomenology, and site-specific performance, to name but three cognate areas of study. Just as theatrical space is no longer only the scenographer's territory, so too it is no longer possible to talk about space in performance without overlapping a variety of methodologies and disciplines. In the pages ahead, I'll first explore a range of historical and contemporary approaches to space and place in theatre and performance, before offering three clarifying case studies that interleave these approaches in an effort to generate rich political readings.

In Section One, after a brief discussion of theatrical space in relation to historical dramatic theory and an introduction to the work of key modern thinkers Henri Lefebvre, Edward Soja, and Doreen Massey, I will discuss three frameworks that use a blend of interdisciplinary methods to make sense of theatrical space as imaginative and hopeful, as concrete and material, and as pragmatic—as a function of dramaturgy. These frameworks are: (1) urban performance studies, as it intersects with urban theory on the one hand and performance studies on the other; (2) genre, in particular modern realism, which I will argue is not simply a means of dramatic organization, but also crucially *an orientation in space*; and (3) theatre as "contact zone," a space of world-making that aims to bridge divided spaces (e.g., between audiences and artists, or between participants of different genders, classes, or skin colors) and to excavate the hidden or neglected memories of specific, concrete places. Along the way, I will introduce us to a range of tools, including from human geography, from cultural materialism, from phenomenology, and from acting theory, alongside the organizing notions of the "topographic" stage, the "haunted" stage, and more.

In Section Two, three case studies will allow us to test the theoretical frameworks I describe in Section One as tools for spatial critique, and to demonstrate how multiple methods of spatial analysis can be deployed together to create rich, dense readings of spatial politics on the stage. My first case study looks at Platform's urban audio walk *And While London Burns* (2007), exploring the spaces of the city as simultaneously "stage" and "auditorium," a place of money, power, and ecological disaster that is deeply felt in our bodies as we navigate real place in real time along with the audio track playing on our headphones (for more on "headphone" theatre, please see *Theory for Theatre Studies: Sound* by Susan Bennett). My second case study takes up *Fräulein Julie* (2010), Katie Mitchell's adaptation of Strindberg's *Miss Julie* that uses cinema technology to place both onstage and backstage spaces in front of its audiences simultaneously, encouraging a meditation on the ways gendered labor shapes, and is shaped by, the spaces of both the kitchen and the stage. Finally, my third case study, *The Shipment* (2009) by Young Jean Lee's Theatre Company, will let us think about how space makes race: it shows us how racism and White privilege depend upon the reproduction of certain normative spatial structures for their violent power—in the "real" world but also, importantly, at the theatre.

My goal in the book's first two sections is to demonstrate how new political readings of theatre and performance events can emerge from an eclectic blend of established approaches to theatrical space. In Section Three, however, I leave these entirely behind and ask us to think about how such established approaches themselves may entrench particular kinds of normative spaces—the space of our learning about space at the theatre; the very nature of ownership over space at the theatre. I will argue that un-learning such approaches (by thinking meta-critically about the world-making power of theory itself) may help lead us, eventually, to the decolonization of the so-called "Western" stage—a space historically, as it remains now, owned and inhabited very unequally. In this final section, I'll talk a bit about "settler colonialism" as a pervasive but often under-recognized spatial technology in countries across the globe, from Peru, New Zealand, and Australia to Finland, the United Kingdom, the United States, and Canada. I will then argue that the project of reconciliation and redress, in the wake of colonialism's ongoing, violent present, offers one essential future focus for space- and place-making at the theatre—for artists, critics, and audiences all. To conclude by way of example, I will share my experience of viewing *Kiinalik: These Sharp Tools*, a 2017 collaborative performance lecture by settler Canadian artist Evalyn Parry and Inuk artist Laakkuluk Williamson Bathory. As I do so, I'll borrow extensively (with permission) from a collaboratively written reflection on the show that I created with London-based author and activist So Mayer. Our shared words will (I hope) demonstrate that, when it comes to reckoning with the political power of the stories space tells, multiple perspectives will always be preferable to one.

SECTION ONE

Methodologies and Approaches

The Back Story: The Spaces of Classical Dramatic Theory

Before I turn to several of the routes into theatrical space and place established in the twentieth century, we should consider briefly some of the ways dramatic theory has historically conceptualized space, both on and off stage. While the late-twentieth-century "spatial turn" is now a scholarly commonplace, considerations of space and place at the theatre—practical, political, and above all philosophical—lie at the heart of Western debates about mimesis since the writings of Aristotle.[1]

Aristotle's famous definition of tragedy in the *Poetics* includes a number of practical injunctions that frame tragedy as primarily a spatial art form. First, he argues that tragedy is "the imitation of an action"; he notes that this action must be "serious and ... complete in itself," that it should take "dramatic, not ... narrative form," and that its object is to arouse cathartic reactions in spectators and listeners (2000: 49). As he prescribes the compositional elements of tragedy, Aristotle mentions first the importance of spectacle ("the stage appearance of the actors"), following this with "melody" and "diction," among others (49–50). This might be unexpected; we often think of Aristotle as giving primary importance to the written, and not the staged, tragic work, as he focuses on matters of decorum, probability, and the power of tragedy to teach us moral lessons. In fact, not long after he gives spectacle pride of place in the list of elements above, he contradicts himself to claim that spectacle is only "an attraction," that it is not actually required for tragic effect, and that stage performance is ultimately "the least artistic of all the parts" of a tragedy, the purview of "the costumier" rather than "the poet" (51). The contradiction is telling, though—because despite his main interest in dramaturgical prescription and his wavering over the importance of spectacle, throughout the *Poetics* Aristotle returns again and again to emphasize embodied action on stage as a major part of the process of conveying tragic meaning. He insists that all aspects of tragedy must revolve around the imitation of an action and that such an imitation in tragedy is ultimately superior to that found in epic poetry precisely because it gives pleasure in its musical and spectacular dimensions *as well as* in its written or spoken form (it can be enjoyed both "as read" and "as acted," making it versatile, diverse, and delightful in comparison [67]).

What can we make of Aristotle's ambivalence over performance? In part, the apparent contradictions in the *Poetics* result from the fragmentary nature of the documents we retain; we know Aristotle largely through his translators and interpreters, and so we cannot fully know "his" perspective on these matters at all. The contradictions also result from Aristotle's somewhat peculiar place in Greek dramatic history, as he interprets the classical Greek tragedy of the fifth century BC (the period of Aeschylus, Euripides, and Sophocles) through the lens of his own, much more spectacle-driven fourth-century theatre culture (Gerould 2000: 44). But Aristotle's contradictions, and the sometimes-confusing ambiguities they generate in his text, also reveal something else, something that significantly undergirds Aristotle's influence on Renaissance and early modern European theatre theorists.

This "something else" is an implicit understanding that drama in performance, as an event that appears live in one time and one place for the benefit of a group of public viewers, must inevitably negotiate the shared, collective spaces inhabited by the many stakeholders who make up what Christopher Balme calls the "theatrical public sphere" (2014): actors and creators; citizens; competition judges and politicians; as well as those of lesser sociopolitical status, including laborers, women, and (in Aristotle's time) slaves. For Aristotle, the imitation of a complete, "probable" action leading to the cathartic purging of emotion makes its required impact on audience members only when it *takes place* before them; further, Aristotle argues that such "taking place" can and should happen both in the physical spaces of the theatre (onstage; offstage) and in spectators' imaginations (hence the value of tragedy over epic poetry). When crafting a work of tragedy (or any work) for the stage, however, the matter of "taking place" becomes infinitely more complex than it is when the spaces of a narrative are merely imagined by a solitary reader. For how does a playwright, or an actor, or a costumier (or a theorist!) guarantee that the spectacle's stimuli will reach audience members as intended, and translate into hoped-for emotional reactions or moral lessons? How does one get the messages of staged tragedy to traverse the space *between* spectacle and spectator effectively? These issues ghost the *Poetics*; the prospect of shaping a shared performance/reception space proper to arousing catharsis thus becomes an unspoken, but essential, goal of Aristotle's tragic theory. It also becomes a problem that will reverberate through the centuries of theatre theory that follow him.

Aristotle's emphasis on not just action but on a "unity" of action at the heart of successful tragedy produces one of his most important spatial legacies. The notion that a play must be contained and complete in its represented action led, in the writings of Aristotle's Renaissance interpreters, to the idea that a play should also exhibit a unity of place—i.e., that a piece of theatre should not locate itself in more physical places than an audience can reasonably imagine characters inhabiting or traversing for the period of time represented by the action on stage. As Arnold Aronson helpfully reminds us, however, the sense of space and time that saturated Aristotle's own theatre-going moment was capacious, and nothing in the *Poetics* prescribes a unity of time or place on the stage—only unity of action (see Aronson 2013: 86, 89). Indeed, the controversial French playwright Pierre Corneille, writing of the "three unities" in his third dramatic treatise at the height of the neoclassical period in France (*c.* 1660), also notes that neither Aristotle nor the influential Greco-Latin poet Horace (following Aristotle) advocate specifically for a unity of place (see also Gobert 2013: 226, n. 20). Nevertheless, Corneille associates a potential spatial injunction with the "rule" of the unity of time derived from Aristotle: that a play's action should take place over no more than twenty-four hours, and therefore clearly should not include travel to places one could not reach in twenty-four hours (Corneille 2000: 164). Corneille, like many of Aristotle's early European interpreters, isn't especially orthodox in his adherence to the unities as he juggles both Aristotle's expectations and the vicissitudes of his own, very different cultural context (maybe it's twenty-four hours, he writes, or maybe it's two; maybe it's whatever ground you've covered on your horse in two hours, or maybe it's whatever locales you believe your audience can handle given the strictures of the narrative [164–5]). However, the spirit of his adherence best demonstrates the significance of Aristotle's teachings for early modern European theatrical culture. Dramatic theory in the wake of Aristotle focuses on the logistical challenges of creating structural unity within a dramatic narrative, and that unity is intended to operate in the service of making the stage-world, once realized before an audience, appear as realistic, as believable, and thus often as conservative as possible.[2] "Believability" assumes a shared belief system in which everyone invests; it is thus meant to limit the range of potential spectatorial reactions to the theatre event. Unity on stage, in effect, is designed to keep all stakeholders present at the drama *in the same place*—physically, psychically, and socially—while they act, or while they watch. Writes Aronson: on the neoclassical stage, governed by a precise, mathematical sense of perspective, "everything had to coalesce into a single, unified, exclusive image" (2013: 88).

Unity leads to recognizability, to believability, to "probability"; these things in turn lead to clear and focused limits on and in stage space, both literal and imagined. Insisting on "unity" as central to dramatic creation also means delimiting, before a dramatic work is even conceived or a performance imagined, what worlds might be permitted to players in or viewers of a performance: "unity" at its most basic means that not all places, experiences, or ideas (anything outside the "uni"-verse of permissible imaginings) should be available for exploration, scrutiny, or enjoyment at the theatre. Corneille writes that to invoke too many places over the course of a tragedy is to "demand an extraordinary attention of the spectator," and thus to distract them from "taking a real pleasure" in the performance (159): here he equates a spectator's imagining of places beyond the scope of the immediate story on stage with distraction rather than joy. It bears noting, however, that Corneille wrote his three treatises on dramatic literature under the watchful eye of the culture police at the Académie Française, a neoclassical body that was rigorous in its insistence on adherence to classical unity, and to whose sanction he (as a dramatist who had previously, and infamously, skirted the rules) was particularly vulnerable (Aronson 2013: 87; Gobert 2013: 51). What Corneille offers us in this statement on unity of place, then, is not simply an injunction against too wide a stage-world, but a *state-sanctioned*, politically motivated injunction against too wide a stage-world. The hand of government appears behind him as academicians argue over whether or not both Paris and Rouen can be shown in the same performance (and over what such free-range representation might mean, especially for ordinary spectators not used to envisioning a world beyond their local communities and basic needs). In their somewhat unexpected (to us, anyway) spatial politics Corneille and the Académie also follow Aristotle, however: the *Poetics* is deeply invested in the subtle but important difference between representing what "is" and what "ought to be" at the theatre. Aristotle writes, for example, "a likely impossibility is always preferable to an unconvincing possibility. The story should never be made up of improbable incidents; *there should be nothing of the sort in it*" (2000: 64, my emphasis). What worlds, the Aristotelian strand of dramatic theory finally asks, *should* be sanctioned as *possible* at the theatre? Which worlds should remain off-limits to our imaginings—and why?

Of course, not everyone writing dramatic theory after Aristotle is interested in supporting the spatial politics of stage unity. Ironically, Corneille's 1637 play *Le Cid* served as one source of the very rules of French neoclassicism precisely because it transgressed the unities of space and action awkwardly, getting him into a mountain of trouble and conditioning his more hide-bound future self (Gobert 2013: 50–1). Meanwhile, Renaissance writers Philip Sidney in England and Felix Lope de Vega in Spain argued for the social good of various dramatic forms (comedy and tragicomedy among them) precisely because of the space-making they encouraged as they permitted audience imaginations more scope. For Lope, for example, tragicomedy held the potential to reach mass audiences, making the theatre a more socially inclusive space that might allow persons less literate or socially mobile to imagine what it would be like to inhabit worlds other than the ones to which they, in their daily lives, were limited. (In a notorious dig at the Aristotelians, represented by the "Madrid Academy" in his *The New Art of Writing Plays* [1609], Lope writes: "Impossibilities avoid, your duty lies / Only in seeking truthful imitation. / Don't let your lackey speak above his station" [2000: 142–3].) Sidney's *Defense of Poesy* (1583) was written expressly to refute the arguments of a wave of anti-theatrical thinkers who argued that plays were packs of lies devised to distract good English men and women from the real world by encouraging the licentious trying-on of other ways of being and acting (including rowdy, sexually transgressive ways of being and acting—early modern theatres were agitated, joyful, contentious public places). Sidney's defense ultimately names drama, and especially comedy, superior to the disciplines of history and philosophy because, he argues, in its dependence on human imagination lies its ethics: poets do not lie, because they do not *claim* to offer any one, firm truth (as historians and philosophers ostensibly do). They are, by trade, inventors (2000: 123). Notably, Sidney was a proponent of the Aristotelean unities, but with a twist: he regarded them as supporting drama's imaginative powers, not limiting them. Tragedy, he writes, "is tied to the laws of poesy, and not of history"; that means it is "not bound to follow the story, but [has] liberty either to feign a quite new matter or to frame the history to the most tragical conveniency" (125). Drama opens the world up—that is its fictive nature.

In both strands of dramatic theory after Aristotle, then, the structure and function of the theatrical event is tied implicitly to its latent power to stage alternate worlds: to expand the imagined spaces (social, political, creative, or otherwise) to which audience members have access outside the theatre, or to restrict access to those spaces in the name of political continuity or the maintenance of social order. The stage-world itself—the nuts and bolts of where a play takes place, and how that world is rendered in performance—is similarly expanded or restricted depending on the politics of a given dramatist, their patrons, and the pressures brought to bear on them by their sociopolitical contexts. There is one other noteworthy piece to this story, however, because the unification of the stage-world Aristotle and his followers seek drives toward one clear, ultimate goal: catharsis, the experiencing and purging of potentially damaging emotions. Catharsis demands that the (figurative, imaginative, if not the physical) space between spectacle and spectator shrinks to very little: that the sounds, images, and ideas offered in and from onstage spaces simply and directly reach spectators in their auditorium seats, and impact them as intended. Catharsis therefore shows us Aristotle at his most spatially obsessed, and the long legacy of catharsis for dramatic theory reveals the anxiety with which theatre makers have regarded the spaces that bind audience members to performers ever since.

The cathartic duo of pity and fear are typically regarded as safety-valve emotions; we feel them, and we are warned not to contravene the rules that govern our public lives, as Oedipus or Medea or Clytemnestra do (to their peril). Understood this way, catharsis supports a conservative vision of Aristotle's unified, bounded stage world that (sometimes gently, sometimes forcefully) restricts audience imagination about place, time, and the possible, and that ultimately invites us to invest in the social ideals of a stable status quo. Locating cathartic emotion—indeed, locating any emotion at the theatre!—is not quite so simple, though. Aristotle's theory of emotional release is by no means universal, though it is typically reckoned to be; in fact, it is specific to a pre-Christian, fourth-century Greek theatre context, and it is underpinned by two key assumptions based on understandings of human embodiment normal for that context. First, it assumes that the staged spectacle will *seamlessly* create specific, embodied reactions in audience members sitting in the auditorium, at a not insignificant physical distance from actors and action—in other words, that it will *take place* in the stage area, but its physical, spiritual, and social impacts will be felt well beyond that area, along with sounds and vibrations from music and singing, and any effects generated by watching the reactions of (masked) figures moving on stage. Second, it assumes that all spectators in the auditorium space will have *the same* embodied reactions to the events taking place on stage, if those events are carefully controlled, and that those reactions will be pity and fear if the tragedy is properly composed. These assumptions appear in Aristotle's *Poetics* as aspirational declarations, as an "ought to be" whose "is" can be guaranteed by following his compositional rules; those rules themselves, however, reveal in their very necessity the potential volatility of all stage emotions, once set into public circulation in shared actor-audience space.

To understand how the volatility of public emotion—carefully controlled for in Aristotle's theory, and explored extensively by theorists following him—can literally impact the spaces of the stage and the social worlds they reflect and create, let's return one more time to Pierre Corneille. Corneille was not just one of Aristotle's most important European interpreters; he was a theorist writing on the cusp of the theatrical modernity to which we will shortly turn. Via Corneille, we can see quite clearly how dramatic theory's historical investment in both unity and catharsis becomes, when modernity arrives in Europe, the source of a profound spatial instability that results in extraordinary dramaturgical and architectural effects. As R. Darren Gobert (2013) has argued in an important book about the impact of René Descartes on the development of the modern stage, Corneille's moment in history (mid-seventeenth-century France) saw a profound shift in worldview from God-centered to human-centered. Predicated upon Descartes's famous theorization of human subjectivity as individual and interiorized, this new, human-centered worldview required a renovation of the very meaning of the word "catharsis." Gobert notes: "the universal experience of pity and fear theorized by Aristotle cannot be reconciled with an audience of individualized subjects" (12; see also 62). The rules of neoclassicism, however, and the intense pressure to follow them brought to bear on Corneille and his contemporaries by the Académie Française, meant that catharsis was still required of every tragedy that sought to "take place" before an actual audience in pre-revolutionary France. Corneille's solution, Gobert argues, was to develop a "catharsis of wonder" (50)—a much more capacious, individually felt emotion than either "pity" or "fear"—that made room for a wide variety of audience reactions to the tragic spectacle. All of these disparate reactions, however, for Corneille could be reconciled under the Cartesian notion of intersubjective generosity (the idea that individuals operate in an embodied, affective network, not in isolation), and thereby to the rubric of the moral lessons attached to catharsis (to do good; to not take action that leads to harm for others) (54–6, 61).

Wonderment might encompass a vast range of emotional experience at the theatre, yet still drive toward social well-being; in itself, Corneille's vision is conservative in its community orientation. But it is not, like Aristotle's, restrictive in its basic assumptions about the way actor and spectator interact in shared performance space: rather than imagining a straight line from one to another, from intended to "landed" cathartic emotion, Corneille structures his theoretical stage space as a Cartesian network, a rhizomatic circulation of various actions and reactions that might take very different final forms for individual spectating bodies but still lead to similar social ends. He thus reimagines the philosophical space of theatrical communication using a Cartesian understanding of the human mind-body, and he theorizes fully for the first time the powerful space-making potential of the *embodied* human spectator at the theatre (Gobert 2013: 59–60). In this project Corneille is thoroughly modern, and we will see his legacy in the writers and theories we explore ahead in this book. In this project in *his* moment in place and time, however, he was on the controversial vanguard: one of the key material effects of the Cartesian opening-up of theatrical space to complex human experience was a sharpening and tightening of stage space *proper*, the birth of the modern perspectival stage.

Historically, the spaces of the stage, and of the theatre buildings that house it, have taken a wide variety of physical forms (see Wiles 2003), but the stage we as late modern subjects are most used to encountering—the proscenium arch, before a raked auditorium—dates to the moment of Corneille and Descartes. Descartes unleashed the power of the human mind as an active agent in the world; his theories of embodiment led to what later philosophers came to understand as a hierarchical split between mind and body, reason and emotion (represented in Descartes's famous phrase "I think, therefore I am"), and ultimately to the idea of what the twentieth-century philosopher Martin Heidegger called the "world picture." "World picture" refers to the world grasped by a solitary subject looking outward, understanding the spaces around them through their own sense of self.[3] Throughout his path-breaking book, Gobert demonstrates that Descartes in fact prized the *interconnectedness* of individual human subjects, as well as the interdependence of individual subjects' brains and bodies, intellectual and emotional faculties, and that this is the world experience Corneille attempted to stage (Gobert 2013: 155, 159–60). The tug of the neoclassical unities, though, and of the linear structures they imposed upon narratives as well as upon stage and viewing spaces, matched well with an interpretation of Descartes that split mind from body and elevated the former. The result, through the end of the seventeenth century, was the renovation of theatre architecture accordingly: from Renaissance-era spaces that placed spectators in close bodily proximity to both actors and one another, mixing and mingling performance and viewing spaces (129–30), to spaces that "asserted more and more strongly the independence of spectators from spectacle and from one another." Importantly, these spaces prized the creation of "a single, objective viewpoint" for each spectator, paying careful attention to auditorium sightlines so as to elevate the visual above all other sensory encounters with the spectacle (126).

This is the stage we typically know as "modern": the diegetic spaces created by individual set designs are placed into a mimetic stage space built with a geometrical center and a clear vanishing point in mind (Aronson 2013: 88–9). Audience vision tracks inward from the seats in the rake, from various viewing points (restricted or unrestricted: check your tickets), and not the other way around (try glancing beyond the footlights, from the stage). Audience members' subjective viewpoints govern the objective realities on stage; the "ought to be" of the narrative is confirmed as "is" through our eyes. The unified worldviews we often ascribe to the realist drama of the late nineteenth century are thus spatially dependent, spatially aware—and also spatially malleable. Because whatever the architects, set designers, playwrights, or philosophers of perspectivalism may intend, human emotion remains circulatory (see Ahmed 2004), and spectatorial reactions remain devilishly unpredictable, productive as well as consumptive. Surveying an early English perspectival stage, Gobert writes:

> The "objective" spectator at a theater like the Queen's Theatre in the Haymarket might well be situated at zero point, his eyes trained along a perspectival line. But what such spectators watch is transformed by their watching, since the nonreproducible and fundamentally emotional exchange between actor and audience inevitably colors the performance. We do well, too, to remember that visual perceptions are for Descartes representational ... mobilizing "the performative quality of all seeing," in Peggy Phelan's formulation. (2013: 160)

However we may, as viewers, be trained by the spaces we encounter at the theatre to regard, react to, or assess extant political or social models, the theatre remains a place where human actions, reactions, and emotions crisscross, and can transform, social space in unexpected ways. As a plastic art form driven by collective human imagination, the theatre makes fresh "space" from a bunch of bodies gathered in a shared time and place: it puts our collective worldviews into circulation, locating them for a time among the participants in the spectacle, in the spaces we inhabit together. Any single creator's ability to curb or shape that circulation is limited by the irreducible power of spectators' embodied, intersubjective experiences of what they see, hear, and feel, live in the moment.

Though Aristotle did not understand the human body's space-making potential as we do (Gobert 2013: 60), he betrays anxiety about the control of human emotions at the theatre in his careful prescriptions for the generation of pity and fear; after all, a great deal is at stake in theatre's potential social effects. David Wiles notes that ancient Greek theatre, long associated with democratic practice, is also driven by sacred rites and that the playing spaces of the theatres of Dionysus (in Athens) and Ikarion (in the mountain village of the same name) were originally built to create a physical link between the representation of the god in the temple adjacent, and the space of performance beyond it, not radically unlike the modern, perspectival stage I just described—though in this case directed toward ritualistic ends (Wiles 2003: 28–30). This historical association of theatrical space with religious practice reminds us that, in cultures governed by specific and carefully policed relationships to higher powers, powers understood to delimit and hierarchize the human world and restrict human potential, the ownership and control of *all* public spaces—not just performance spaces—are paramount to the maintenance of order. Those afraid of theatre's power to imagine *other worlds than the given one*—worlds in which those who do not currently enjoy freedom might do, or worlds in which those who currently have no power could have—are, in fact, actually staking a claim to theatre's latent, potentially transgressive, even dangerous spatial potential.

Twentieth-century theatre and performance theory takes seriously the political implications of the historical injunctions against making new worlds at the theatre, and understands theatre's ability to mobilize new spaces among and between human bodies as its most profound ethical, and its most progressive political, power. Let's turn to the work of this theory now.

Contemporary Lens #1: Theatre and the Production of Social Space

Cultural Materialism and the "Spatial Turn" in Theatre Studies

Historical theorists recognized the theatre's power as a social and political tool that could have significant real-world impact;

nevertheless, they tended to concentrate their commentary on that power inside the theatre building, and often on the events on stage or inside the structures of narrative. While very well aware of theatre's larger embeddedness in the public sphere and its beholding to social mores, these theorists preferred to account for theatre's social effects by looking inward, at the formal dimensions of the drama, rather than outward at the warp and weft of its contextualizing material circumstances. A number of modern critics, as I indicated in the introduction and as we will see a little later in this section, take a similar trajectory, reading dramatic structure as essential to theatre's space-making capacity. However, one of the most influential developments in theatre and performance theory over the last century has been the rise of cultural studies, and in particular cultural materialism, which allows critics to make sense of theatrical meaning by examining in close detail a theatre building's or company's larger social, geographical, political, and economic contexts.

Before we go any further, we need to understand what is meant by "cultural materialism." The term refers to an interdisciplinary methodology that explores the ways in which different cultural phenomena are enmeshed with one another at the level of lived, material experience, and it attempts to account for the tangible effects of that enmeshment on the circulation of goods, money, labor, and ideas. Cultural materialism understands "culture" as quotidian—i.e., as "ordinary"—rather than as "highbrow" or "lowbrow"; that means it attaches no moral value to the idea of culture, but instead includes under its umbrella "all the practices and objects that make up 'a whole way of life'" (Harvie 2009: 23). Cultural materialism is as interested in the street-level interactions of young people, for example, as it is in so-called "elite" pursuits like attending the opera. It regards these two phenomena as related rather than discrete; it does not hierarchize them, but instead explores the impact they might have on each other as constituent parts of a larger social context. In her 2013 book *Fair Play: Art, Performance and Neoliberalism*, Jen Harvie writes:

> I understand culture as always enmeshed in social, material and historical conditions; contributing to the production of Ideologies and therefore important to consider in the construction of social relations, especially hierarchies of class. A cultural materialist approach emphasizes that cultural practices such as art and performance do not exist in some kind of material and historical vacuum ... Its examination of cultural practices as processes in material contexts consistently aims to explore culture as a site of ideological contest, and to consider the ways that culture participates in the dissemination of ideologies. (2013: 16)

When Harvie speaks in the above quotation about the production of ideologies, she is referencing cultural materialism's ability to account for *how* ideological valuations of cultural phenomena come to take hold in our imaginations. Cultural materialism doesn't much care whether the opera was "good," or whether or not the young people skateboarding in a carpark are "up to no good"; instead, it asks what those very terms ("good"; "no good") mean in a given context, what kinds of value inflections they carry, and what ideological as well as material effects those inflections generate (e.g., banning loitering around important civic buildings like the opera house).

Cultural materialism therefore explores what two groups of cultural consumers (e.g., opera-goers and street-level gamers) sharing the same relative space (e.g., a city's downtown core) can tell us about the ideological, social, and economic forces at work in that space, about whom they benefit, and about how they reproduce and reinforce those (often unequal) benefits on a daily basis. In *Theatre & The City*, Harvie names "space, institutional structures and practices, money and people" as the "material conditions" of theatrical meaning-making she will consider. She writes: "These features address where theatre takes place in the city and what that place means; how its architecture signifies; what economies it participates in; and what its demographics are—who works in theatre, in what conditions, and who spends their leisure time there" (2009: 24–5). Notice not only that "space" is the first term here, but also how spatially resonant the rest of Harvie's description is. For Harvie, cultural materialism *is* a spatial practice, and an ideal means of making sense of social space in relation to theatrical space.[4]

Harvie is only one of many contemporary theorists who use cultural materialist methodologies to understand the "place" of theatre and performance practices in today's world. In the relatively early book *Places of Performance: The Semiotics of Theatre Architecture* (1989), Marvin Carlson links the rise of cultural materialism as a methodology to the emerging (at that time) spatial turn in theatre studies; as he does so, Carlson captures nicely the stakes of the shift from insular and formal dramaturgical analysis to interdisciplinary, materialist analysis for a deep understanding of theatrical space and place. He writes:

> No longer do we necessarily approach theatre primarily as the physical enactment of a written text with our historical concern anchored in the interplay between that text and its physical realization. We are now at least equally likely to look at the theatre experience in a more global way, as a sociocultural event ... Such a change of focus requires also a change in the way we look at the places where theatrical performance occurs, which may or may not be traditional theatre buildings. ... The entire theatre, its audience arrangements, its other public spaces, its physical appearance, even its location within a city, are all important elements of the process by which an audience makes meaning of its experience. (2)

Carlson is, among other things, a historian of theatre theory; his invocation of past approaches at the top of this quotation might ring a bell. Writing specifically about place in this book, and using cultural materialism as a tool to assist in the close reading of the sign systems that give theatre architecture meaning (what the "semiotics" of his title means), he is able to account for the way spaces *outside* the theatre impact meaning-making *inside* the theatre, as well as between "text and its physical realization"—the things that Aristotle, Corneille, and their peers were primarily obsessed with. To put this differently, we might say that cultural materialism is not just a spatial practice (as I noted above): it is defined by its braiding together of the social and the spatial at all levels of analysis, and it thus offers contemporary theatre and performance scholars the tools to account carefully, and even perhaps objectively, for the world-making potential that early dramatic theorists recognized in the theatre but also often feared about it. Cultural materialism also offers us, today, the power to recognize, name, and deconstruct the forces—political, aesthetic, economic, philosophical—that can limit theatre's world-making potential in unexpected, often invisible, and sometimes dangerous ways.

Human Geography and the "Social Turn": Henri Lefebvre, Edward Soja and Doreen Massey

At the same time that theatre and performance studies were steadily being influenced by cultural materialist analysis in the latter part of the twentieth century, scholars working in the field known as human geography were asking similar questions about how populations and the spaces they occupy interact and influence one another's development. This branch of geography, like the cultural materialism to which it is connected, investigates how social forces operate in concert with both human communities and their physical surroundings in order to produce the very thing we call "space." Critically, human geography understands human activity and the conditions that contextualize it as central to the creation of space and place—it does not regard space or place as pre-given, or preexisting, society. In this core understanding, human geography has had enormous influence on cultural studies as an area of academic investigation, on cultural materialism as a scholarly methodology, and also on the spatial turn in theatre and performance studies.

In *The Production of Space*, first published in 1974 and translated into English in 1991, Henri Lefebvre makes two critical claims. First, he argues that "(social) space is a (social) product," one that "serves as a tool of thought and of action" and that "in addition to being a means of production ... is also a means of control, and hence domination, of power" (26). Lefebvre notes that some of his readers may find this argument obvious, but only because they imagine "social space" to be bounded by social activities, and thus to be distinguishable from both physical space (the "given" space of the earth, let's say) and "mental space" (as defined by "philosophers and mathematicians"—the space of abstract imagination). The social space Lefebvre has in mind encompasses both of these formations but is not limited to either: it cannot be reduced to a physical form, nor to an abstract void framed by ideology (27). "Social space" in Lefebvre's conception is not simply the space in which human social interaction *takes place*; rather, social space is the entirety of human perception, activity, imagination, and social organization, produced in relation to economic, political, historical, and ideological formations.

Lefebvre's second central claim is perhaps even more important. If social space is a social product, he notes, it is also not readily visible as such. The routine, continuous production of space by social actors (both institutional, like governments, and individual, like you and me) is concealed in order to maintain the smooth operations of power. This concealment is the result of two "illusions": what Lefebvre calls the "illusion of transparency" on the one hand (the idea that space is a "given," where private thought can simply and directly be translated into realized, public action), and "the realistic illusion" on the other (where space is assumed to be "natural"—because it is the physical reality in which we live) (27–9). These illusions work together, Lefebvre claims, to create our commonsense, simplistic notion of the relationship between human bodies and the spaces they inhabit: the idea that "space" is "free of traps or secret places" (28), free of depth or complexity in itself—that it is *where we work*, not something that we work on, or that *works on us*. Lefebvre's challenge to geography, and indeed to the broader field of critical social theory, lies in his central argument that this spatial "innocence" is in fact no more than a comforting illusion itself, one that hides from us the most complex operations of power in the public sphere.

As both a philosopher and a cultural materialist, Lefebvre builds his arguments about social space in part by engaging with a history of ideas, and with the ways in which space has been made comprehensible—too simply comprehensible, as he claims—by that history. This is also the project of Edward Soja, an American geographer, urban theorist, and ardent follower of Lefebvre. In his 1989 book *Postmodern Geographies: The Reassertion of Space in Critical Social Theory*, Soja brings Lefebvre's arguments (at this point, not yet translated into English) about the social production of social space into conversation with French philosopher and historian Michel Foucault's definition of "heterotopia" (which we will consider a bit later in this section). Soja does this principally in order to re-evaluate the entrenched bias against geography (perceived as no more than the study of "given" space) and toward history (perceived as the study of historical oppressions and the workings of power in society) in twentieth-century social theory. Reframing geography and history—space and time—as not just aligned but collaborative areas of investigation, Soja writes:

> Just as space, time, and matter delineate and encompass the essential qualities of the physical world, spatiality, temporality, and social being can be seen as the abstract dimensions which together comprise all facets of human existence. More concretely specified, each of these abstract existential dimensions comes to life as a social construct which shapes empirical reality and is simultaneously shaped by it. ... How this ontological nexus of space-time-being is conceptually specified and given particular meaning in the explanation of concrete events and occurrences is the generative source of all social theory. (25)

Soja builds on this influential argument in his 1996 book *Thirdspace*, as he theorizes a new framework for understanding the interconnections of space, time, and history in social and political thought. The term "thirdspace" is Soja's shorthand for the new critical perspective he advocates; it adds the "socio-spatial" as well as the "socio-temporal" (i.e., consideration of how time and place are both connected to, and products of, social formations) to the "traditional core of Western thought, which focused primarily on the relation ... between history and society" as solo, independent concepts (qtd. in Borch 2002: 113). "Thirdspace" allows scholars and critics to understand, for example, how class identity is not only a product of historical oppression—of one's "place" in time—but also a product of one's locational identity—one's literal "place" in the world.

Both Lefebvre and Soja were interested not just in social space, but in the spaces of modernity—which means they were interested in urban space, as Anglo-European cities grew rapidly and their cultural make-up changed extraordinarily through the long twentieth century. Doreen Massey, a British feminist geographer, has been among the most important theorists to take up Lefebvre's and Soja's legacy in urban studies; in *Space, Place, and Gender* (1994), *For Space* (2005), and *World City* (2007, rev. 2010), she moves beyond the traditional Marxist focus on class identity in human geography to examine how gender, racial, and other cultural identities (such as those keyed to disability) interleave in the shaping of modern, global urbanism. This move makes Massey's work influential not only in geography, urban studies, and cultural studies, but also in critical race studies, feminist theory, and gender studies.

In *For Space*, Massey proffers her own addition to the socio-spatial framework I discuss above, pioneered by Lefebvre in his equation social space = social product and complicated by Soja's articulation of a "thirdspace" for social theory. She opens the book with three related "propositions": first "that we recognise space as the product of interrelations; as constituted through interactions, from the immensity of the global to the intimately tiny"; second "that we understand space as the sphere of the possibility of the existence of multiplicity in the sense of contemporaneous plurality"; and third "that we recognise space as always under construction" (9). In her introduction to *World City* (2007) two years later, she elaborates the stakes of these propositions, demonstrating how space works as a political force (especially in large urban centers) today:

> London is … a field of multiple actors, trajectories, stories with their own energies—which may mingle in harmony, collide, even annihilate each other. … That recognition of multiple trajectories is one implication of taking space seriously. It forces respect for the coeval. Many political cosmologies, in contrast, are framed in such a way that "others" (other actors, other trajectories) are in one way or another either obscured from view or relegated to some sort of minority or inferior status. Such cosmologies refuse the challenge of space. (22–3)

Space, Massey argues, is "the dimension of contemporaneous existence" (2007: 23)—a rich field in which "self" and "other" are not constituents in a violent binary, but rather are in it together, along with a host of other (often ignored) actors. Yet, as she argues throughout *For Space* and *World City*, it is also very easy to perceive space as a transparent surface (Lefebvre's illusionary "given"), a backdrop against which political relations play out, with some succeeding while others fail, seemingly as a result of their own independent merits or lack thereof. For Massey, more effective social and political analysis requires us to pay careful attention to what she calls "geographical imaginations": "powerful elements in the armoury of legitimation of political strategies" (24–5), strategies such as those that pit geographical regions (e.g., North vs. South) one against another for a finite pool of riches (20). Thus, "thinking the spatial in a particular way" can either reinforce unequal social and political status quos, or it "can shake up the manner in which certain political questions are formulated" (2005: 9)—questions such as "If actions and policies adopted within one place negatively affect people elsewhere, what responsibility is involved, and what accountability? If a place's very character is integral to sets of relations at the other end of which is produced poverty or deprivation, how should this be addressed?" (2007: 15).

Urban Performance Studies

Cultural materialism offers theatre and performance studies tools for situating theatrical production and consumption firmly in lived space; human geography provides a theoretical backbone for understanding the relational quality of that space, and the often-uneven roles played by social actors in existing social spaces. It's perhaps no surprise, then, that theatre scholars have used these compatible methodologies to look in a granular way at the significance of where, exactly, theatres are located, and what impact "location," in all of its social complexity, has on the work made there. While plenty of notable theatres can be found in semi-rural (or, what we might still imagine to be semi-rural) spaces—in the village of Bayreuth in Germany; in the towns of Stratford-upon-Avon, UK, and Stratford, Ontario, Canada, to name just three well-known examples—we live on an increasingly urban planet, and the majority of theatre buildings are today found in cities.[5] Just as Soja and Massey have used the insights of Lefebvre specifically to revaluate modern global urbanism, then, many scholars of theatre studies' spatial turn work today on performance in the city.

Materialist and geographical approaches have had a significant impact on the rise of reading theatre in/and the city, which forms one key trend in the late modern "spatial turn," but another important contribution to this rise comes from performance studies, a unique discipline that dates back to the 1960s and 1970s (see Schechner and Kirschenblatt-Gimblett, both in Bial 2003). Performance studies reads everyday phenomena as performative acts, the significance of which can be understood using the tools of theatre and performance criticism. Drawing from social anthropology, religious studies, theatre studies, and more, performance studies treats the "culture" ("all the practices and objects that make up 'a whole way of life'") in cultural materialism *as inherently theatrical.* Just as cultural materialism and human geography give the tools of socio-spatial analysis to theatre and performance criticism, so too performance studies gives cultural materialism and human geography the tools of performance analysis to help make sense of how social spaces and their inhabitants "act" together in order to produce the complex interrelations that, for Massey and others, constitute space itself. This powerful methodological blending has, since the early 1990s, coalesced into the development of a sub-discipline called urban performance studies.

Scholars of urban performance examine how both ordinary and purpose-built spaces in the city operate as stages for many different kinds of "acting," both formal and informal, both aesthetically and socially oriented. For example, these scholars might look at parkour and urban gaming, street festivals, or psychogeography practices like urban discovery walks, to name just a few possible subjects (Levin and Solga 2009; Marla Carlson 2009). They might also track the rise of purpose-built theatre venues, as well as theatre or entertainment "districts," examining public policy, urban governance, and real estate trends to understand why, how, and where those districts appear, and how global economic trends impact their development (Bennett 2005, 2013; Levin and Solga 2009; Knowles 2017; McKinnie 2007, 2009, 2017). Regardless of their primary subject matter, however, most urban performance critics begin their research with similar questions. How does a city represent itself—to itself, its citizens, the world? Whose performances define the workings of a given city, and whose are marginalized as "other" to the identity a city wishes to project? How does a city's local theatrical ecology influence its social and economic positioning? What kinds of feelings do urban performances generate, and what are the effects of their circulation?

Walking in the City, Playing in the City

Urban performance studies traces its historical roots to philosopher Walter Benjamin's *Arcades Project* (1927–40), a large and important collection of essays on Parisian city life that imagined the urban wanderer, called the *flâneur*, as the central figure in civic performance. Another key mid-century influence is Guy Debord, one of the founders of a group of European intellectuals called the Situationist International. Like Benjamin's *Arcades Project*, Debord's *The Society of the Spectacle* (1967) theorizes the relationships among people, images, and things (or commodities) in a modern urban culture shaped by an often-overriding impulse to observe and consume, rather than to act and engage. Both of these seminal early volumes provoke important questions for contemporary urban performance scholars. Who gets to "act and engage" in the modern city, and who can only spectate? Who is *privileged* to spectate—to watch and listen, perhaps without being noticed? What difference do criteria like gender, race, or class make to one's potential as an urban performer? When is performing in the city a matter of art and craft, and when is it about bare survival?

Benjamin's *flâneur*, or urban wanderer, nicely telescopes these queries. Exploring how the *flâneur* has been idealized in much city literature as a figure who materializes modern urban space through his travels around and observations of the city, Massey persuasively argues that women are implicitly excluded from this socio-spatial formation, as they have not historically been, and in many places are still not, free to wander the city driven only by creative curiosity (1994: 234). For a woman—as for other racialized or minoritized subjects, including those who are disabled—walking in the city is never a matter simply of art or philosophy; it's also very much about safety and security. Women and minority walkers are not traditionally free to "gaze" wherever they wish as they walk—an important component of Benjamin's theorization of the *flâneur* as one who watches, learns, and is creatively inspired by consuming the images of others on the streets. Instead, they are traditionally gazed upon while on the streets, and the gazes they receive can be disquieting, discriminatory, and even violent (or a precursor to violence). Following Massey and other feminist geographers and cultural critics, urban performance studies maps urban denizens in their gendered and raced as well as class and ability contexts in order to account for the effects of multiple differences, in ways Benjamin and Debord (as well as Lefebvre and Soja) were unable, earlier in the modern period, to do.

My titular phrase "walking in the city" comes from French critic Michel de Certeau's key essay of the same name (in *The Practice of Everyday Life*, 1984), in which he reflects on New York City from two different visual vantage points: from up high atop the World Trade Center and on the street below. De Certeau's distinction between the view of the city "from above" and that "from below" has been central to urban performance studies, particularly as it regards the performance labor of ordinary citizens who, simply in the act of walking around in and using city spaces every day, help to shape the broad, evolving stage their city is always becoming. The idea that individuals are performers on the stage of everyday life, central to both performance studies and urban performance studies, is underpinned by the theory of performativity, first developed by linguist J. L. Austin in the mid-twentieth century, and complicated by philosopher Judith Butler in the 1990s. A performative utterance *does* something: its words are actors, not observers.[6] For de Certeau, urban walking is a kind of performative speech act (97–8): both following and breaking the planned trajectories of a city's streets is akin to using, and adapting, one's own urban language, shifting the framework of the ur-language (the official map or plan) over time. Everyone in the city, from the mayor to the commuter to the homeless person, affects the material flows of city life by virtue of their basic human capacity for quotidian performative acts both linguistic (spoken) and gestural (movement). These acts may be relatively value-neutral: taking an off-grid shortcut to work may eventually mean that shortcut enters the official city plan if enough people use it; a needle disposal bin may appear when city staff realizes addicts are using a particular park at night. However, they may also bear ideological weight: the shortcut may be roped off if private property owners object to its use; gates may be installed at the park if neighbors complain about the presence of drug users.

One of the most prominent ways in which quotidian urban performance registers for scholars of urban performance studies is through street festivals, such as the popular *Nuit Blanche* (an all-night art festival that takes place in dozens of cities annually). Street festivals are in no way a new invention—students of Shakespeare's day may recognize something of the Royal Entry or Lord Mayor's pageant in them, for example—but they have taken on new importance in the late modern, "creative" city. Street festivals are often arts driven (by theatre, visual art, music, or typically all three), and they aim to animate city streets in pleasurably performative ways. They encourage a wide range of ordinary urban and suburban dwellers, as well as tourists, to take on consciously the role of urban *flâneur*, and through the range of spectacles they offer they aim to ensure a safe, "something for everyone" experience of walking and playing in the city. They encourage visitors to travel into the urban core on subways and buses (or take advantage of designated parking zones set up for the event), and to spend money on food and transport, thus contributing to the city's economy (and ensuring similar events can take place on its streets in the future).

Urban festivals organized by, or in partnership with, civic government are often intended to contribute not only to the urban economy, but also to a city's regional, national, and international reputation as a creative hub. The question of how to transform an ordinary, working urban center into a "creative city" became increasingly important for urban policy makers in the early twenty-first century, thanks to the late-twentieth-century shift away from industrial manufacturing ("Fordism") as the basis of many Western urban economies, and toward finance- (and tourism-) driven economic models (often called "post-Fordist" or "neoliberal"). The "creative city" framework for urban development was made famous by urban studies scholar Richard Florida (2002). Florida's theory argues that cities which place an emphasis on creative labor, as well as on an openness to difference, are much more likely to attract affluent professionals in the post-industrial economic landscape. For Florida, all manner of white-collar workers—from engineers to professors to artists—qualify as "creatives" in the city, but artistic labor is of special value because it can be leveraged regularly and fairly inexpensively to demonstrate a city's concrete and ongoing commitment to "creativity."

Florida's theory has been much critiqued (Peck 2005) precisely because it rests on a questionable division between those citizens whose performances count as "creative" (professionals of various kinds; artists) and those whose performances do not (retail, service, or janitorial workers, for example). Urban performance scholars have been at the forefront of this critique. When they take primarily materialist approaches, their analyses look closely at how the performing arts are mobilized for financial gain in the creative city: for example, how the labor of theatre artists forms part of the project of urban gentrification and renewal, or how the rhetorical privileging of creativity does, or does not, translate into real economic benefits for artists and their local communities. When scholars take primarily performance studies approaches to the critique of the creative city, their analyses often foreground the ways in which urban art projects, both amateur and professional, can help to mobilize individual or community engagement, activating memory and encouraging social justice by opening up ways to experience the city from different points of view.

Let's briefly look at two examples of how these critiques work in practice.[7]

The Theatre Building in the Creative City

Michael McKinnie is a UK-based Canadian critic trained in the cultural materialist tradition. In his 2007 book, *City Stages: Theatre and Urban Space in a Global City*, McKinnie develops what he calls "an urban geography of theatre" (13) by examining closely the relationships among civic planning, the city's unique political economy, real estate trends, and regional and national feeling (among other factors), in order to chart their mutual influences on theatrical production in late-twentieth-century Toronto. McKinnie's goal is to understand how these intersecting market and cultural forces affected the development of individual theatre venues and districts in the city; he is similarly interested in how the creative practices, working conditions, and financial structures supporting Toronto's professional theatre networks operated alongside these forces, impacting them while also being shaped by them in turn.

McKinnie's approach involves in-depth, comparative case study analysis. For example, in his first chapter (25–47) he looks at the development of the St Lawrence Centre for the Arts in Toronto's downtown core in 1967 (Canada's centenary) by comparing the social and material conditions that enabled its building with those of the Ford Centre, which was erected in 1993 in North York, a suburban city north of Toronto, in order to help anchor a new "downtown" there. The core of the chapter involves "thick description" (an important cultural materialist practice) of the historical contexts of each project. McKinnie offers detailed readings of national and transnational market trends and real estate practices affecting the capital investments available for each project; clarification of government and private sector funding models for each; discussion of the geographical and social shifts taking place in the immediate areas at the time of each project's development; and consideration of the civic feelings emerging in relation to each project. His analysis is multiply situated, rooted in materialist economics and geography but borrowing strongly from performance studies approaches to audiences' emotional engagements with place.

This multi-pronged approach allows McKinnie to reveal how "downtowns are sites where the investment of capital [from the welfare state, as well as from private investment] produces both money value and sentimental value that exceed the boundaries of downtown. The benefits of downtown investment accrue beyond its borders and beyond any purely cash measure" (32).

Importantly, for McKinnie—as for many other urban performance scholars (including Levin, Harvie, and Bennett) who take a broadly materialist approach—theatre is not the "solution" to the problems market-driven finance capitalism create for arts workers in the creative city, nor is theatre a panacea to alleviate urban blight (as it may be for Florida and his followers). Instead, as McKinnie shows via his Toronto case studies, theatre organizations tend to have "an ambivalent relationship with the market" that can create both economically affirmative and economically and socially subversive effects. In a 2017 article about Toronto's community performance incubator, The Theatre Centre, McKinnie extends his earlier methodology to account for the ways in which international real estate speculation in Toronto's sought-after West Queen West neighborhood at the beginning of the 2000s supported the redevelopment of this important, inclusive cultural venue, while also further driving the area's rapid gentrification and property price inflation. Throughout this article McKinnie demonstrates how an urban performance studies analysis indebted to both social and urban theory and a rigorous cultural materialism can account for the many civic "goods" offered to (and by) the arts in the creative city, while at the same time noting the ways in which those goods might negatively impact neighborhood diversity and access to affordable housing for those most likely to support local, sustained arts innovation over time.

Performing Urban Memories

Urban performance scholars who work with performance studies methodologies often focus on artist-driven theatre and performance events that make the city their stage. These events might include work made at or about public memorials, site-specific theatre productions at key sites around the city, and audio or guided performance walks, to name just three examples. Scholarship about these kinds of events often emphasizes how they may animate forgotten or invisible spaces within the urban fabric and encourage participants (who can be considered both spectators and actors in many cases, and are often both locals and tourists) to think critically about how the city is staged for us, whose lives it values, and what pleasures and responsibilities adhere to the very simple act of "walking" in the city for every one of us. Readings may foreground the performative production of identity and affect rather than the theatrical event's social and economic context, although materialist considerations are never absent from this work (just as, for example, McKinnie's materialist readings allow him to examine the production of civic feelings in Toronto). Performance studies methodologies allow scholars to approach cultural materialism's important question of "who benefits?" from theatre in the city by gauging a performance event's potential to animate that city—its history, its present, and its future—differently, for spectators already familiar with it as well as for those visitors who come with preformed expectations about it. These methodologies allow critics to focus on a particular event's ability to encourage us to practice walking or acting in the city in unexpected ways, so that we may inhabit, even if only briefly, someone else's urban experience.[8]

Audio walks are among the most frequently discussed of these kinds of urban performance events. Artists producing an audio walk will create a soundtrack that captures the quotidian noises of the area in which the walk is located and then set that soundtrack to a fictional narrative. Music is often part of the story, too. The resulting, multi-layered recording is then made available for public download; auditor-spectators can access it individually and complete the walk on their own time, listening to the soundtrack on personal headphones. Both the individual nature of the walk, and the fact that, with headphones on and strolling down the street, participants may appear at a glance no different from any other walker are significant parts of an audio walk's aesthetic, and both contribute to its goal of rendering participants' sense of the streets briefly and critically unfamiliar. (See *Theory for Theatre Studies: Sound* for more detail on the audio component of these kinds of works.)

Audio walks are often created in response to a galvanizing event, or a pressing urban issue: ecological devastation and financial corruption (*And While London Burns*, which we will examine in detail in Section Two); the destruction of a neighborhood and its way of life (Graeme Miller's *Linked*, 2003); or something as simple as a need to recollect the historical inhabitants of an area undergoing gentrification (the ongoing oral history project *[Murmur]*). Urban audio walks often bear a quality of discovery, with participants moving around the city, guided by the narrative voice on their phones, searching for the "aha!" that rarely comes (or, at least, rarely comes in the form one might expect it to take). They trade on a deep-seated feeling of anticipation, one that propels walkers forward yet surprises them at each turn. With those surprises come new insights into how different urban subjects are, or are not, free to take up space in the city; we might say, with a nod to Massey, that they are a way to practice, in embodied and playful fashion, the heterogeneous interrelations that produce all urban space.

One especially notable walk of this kind is *Her Long Black Hair* (*HLBH*), commissioned in 2005 by New York's Public Art Fund and created by the theatre-and-sound artist team of Janet Cardiff and George Bures Miller. *HLBH* is set in and around New York's Central Park, and it invites participants to inhabit the role of *flâneur* through the eyes and ears of a young woman. It also bears the scars of 9/11 on that city, which means it responds both to large-scale urban trauma (the destruction of the towers down from which de Certeau once imagined gazing) and to the personal-as-political, exploring how such trauma registers on individual bodies and their ordinary civic practices.

In an affecting essay called "Ways to Walk New York After 9/11" (2009 [2006]), performance studies scholar Marla Carlson connects her individual experience of walking *HLBH* to her memories of the morning of September 11, 2001, when she witnessed the sounds and smells of the fall of the twin towers from her apartment in Park Slope, Brooklyn. She then asks how audio walks in the post-9/11 city "trigger acts of remembrance and imagination" that have the power to activate a range of feelings and provoke questions about what cities like New York "mean" to different subjects both in that city and beyond it. Examining the provocative effects of Cardiff and Miller's binaural sonic techniques (quite unique at the time of *HLBH*'s development), Carlson writes: "By recording sound in the space in which one later listens to it, and then causing one to discriminate (with difficulty) between the real and the various recorded types of sound, Cardiff's work insists upon the difference between them" (19). This difference is then marshalled to encourage listener-spectator-actors to pay attention to *where* their reactions to each sound are coming from, what kinds of memories they attach to, and what larger ideological implications both reactions and memories might bear. Thinking about walking with "Janet," Cardiff's narrator, through Central Park, Carlson recalls:

> I remember when the park was dangerous even on a beautiful Saturday afternoon—but that's not my personal memory, based on my experience of Central Park. It's a media-built memory of a time when this wasn't my city ... I can compare it to my similar sense of change for Prospect Park in Brooklyn: although I know that violent attacks still occur in Prospect Park, I no longer feel the danger of unexplored strange territory because I now have direct experience of so many long and peaceful walks there. ... Also useful here is the concept of "postmemory," which Marianne Hirsch and Leo Spitzer describe as passed down within families or cultures, "a secondary, belated memory mediated by stories, images, and behaviors among which [one] grew up ... ."

> *Her Long Black Hair* is loaded with triggers for all three sorts of memory and purposely creates confusion between them. (2009: 19)

This "confusion" Carlson finds "sharpens" her sense of hearing, as well as her sense of reality (19): inside the frame of the audio walk, listeners are at once inside the theatrical event and inside the spaces of the city. During the walk the city is, literally, a kind of stage, but it is also, and always, a space of memory and engagement with others. It would be impossible, on a long audio walk like *HLBH*, to avoid encountering others, even if only through glances, smiles, or accidental touching. It would also, likely, be impossible (as Carlson finds, in her own experience of *HLBH*) to avoid encountering the city's ghosts, real and imagined. The work thus animates the city-stage in ways that require participants to regard it historically, mythologically, and politically, as well as materially and socially. It invites walkers to ask sometimes quite personal, at other times entirely community-oriented, questions about what we know and believe about our urban environment and those who share it with us.

Contemporary Lens #2: Genre and "Topographic" Space

In the rest of this section, I will explore two theatrical forms—modernist realism and site-specific performance—as spatial orientations designed to cue audiences to think critically about themselves and their world while they are inside a theatrical event, watching a play. Before we turn to the special labor accomplished by genre, however, let's leave the larger spaces of the city and enter the theatre together. As I'll briefly explore now, the architecture of theatre buildings encourages audiences to come into their performance spaces in particular ways—

ways that are designed to prepare audiences for the messages embedded in the viewing experiences ahead of them.

Architectural Orientations at Shakespeare's Globe

Consider, for example, Shakespeare's Globe theatre on the Bankside in London. This painstaking, carefully researched reproduction of the original Globe theatre includes a replica stage and auditorium space, which is connected by a stone courtyard area to a separate, modern, teaching and office facility (including a box office area), as well as to the Sam Wanamaker Playhouse, a reproduction of an indoor theatre from the early seventeenth century. This network of spaces offers multiple points of entry to audience members, depending upon the purpose of their visit; each point of entry shapes a visitor's experience to the Globe in different ways.

If you're a roving tourist, and you simply want to see and take photos of the reproduction Globe structure, you might approach the complex via the river-facing steps on the north side (though the gates are shut during a performance). If you are visiting to take in a play, ticket-holders may enter from those same steps, but those still to collect will more likely enter through the main box-office doors on the east side of the modern building, encountering the Globe "organization" before the Globe "theatre" proper. If you are part of a school group attending for a tour, you are likely to enter through the box-office doors, line up in the lobby area, and be guided downstairs into the teaching rooms of the modern building for a brief introductory lecture before being taken to visit the theatre spaces and the exhibition below the theatre. Those visiting only the exhibition may use yet another, separate entrance on the west side of the Thames-facing gates, one that bypasses the reproduction theatre altogether. Meanwhile, everyone is encouraged by the overall layout of the space to visit the gift shop at some point: it is centrally located inside the modern building, near to the theatre and next to the toilets, and it is easily accessible through several doors onto the courtyard. (As the Globe is a private charity, funds from gift shop sales are essential to the continuation of all of its education as well as theatrical programming.)

What do we note as we leave the street and enter the Globe's spaces? First of all, we discover that "The Globe," in its modern iteration, isn't just a theatre: it is also a teaching, tourism, and entertainment facility. It is a public and historical space, but it is also private property. It is an essential part of the Bankside's contribution to London as a "creative" and "global" city today. Yet it is also a facility that situates—that has *always* situated—theatre practice in London as at once outward-looking (glancing out over the river to St Paul's and the financial center, the square-mile City of London) and inward-looking (onto the imagined worlds of its broad, decorated stage). Today, the Globe complex orients us toward the history of theatre-making in modern Britain (we often call Shakespeare and his contemporaries "early modern"), as well as toward the pleasures of spectacle removed (at least somewhat) from tourist hubbub and global commerce. But it also, crucially, orients us toward our fellow spectators—i.e., toward one another as collaborative cultural agents.

As Marvin Carlson explains in his important book about the social and cultural meanings of theatre architecture, "the theatre is in fact one of the most persistent architectural objects in the history of Western culture" (1989: 6), and one whose shifting place in the changing urban landscapes of modernity has helped to chart the changing value of theatre itself—the meanings generated by works *on* the stage, for the world *beyond* the stage (2, 7). Looking at the history of Renaissance theatre building across Europe, Carlson notes that London's first public theatres struggled to gain royal favor, which would have protected them from the "antagonism of the city authorities" suspicious about what they were up to; this political conundrum led companies to build immediately outside the city walls, just far enough out of London "proper" to be jurisdictionally free, but close enough that patrons could walk to their shows (68). Companies with some royal favor chose to build on the Thames's south bank for similar reasons (101). The public theatres' patrons included members of the working classes who would not normally be privileged to attend performances in royal spaces such as Whitehall, and whose theatrical inclinations were often linked, in the imagination of their social superiors, to moral failings. Carlson cites Andrew Marvell as the latter comments on an Italian performance at Whitehall in 1675, which (unusually) charged admission and welcomed all patrons who could pay: "All Sorts of People flocking thither, and paying their Mony as at a common Playhouse," he wrote. Sniffing at the spatial incursion of those with cash but no status, he added: "Nay even a twelve-penny Gallery is builded for the convenience of his Majesty's poorer Subjects" (49).

Theatres like the original Globe were commercial ventures that offered scope for adventure and discovery to those limited in both in their daily lives in a stratified culture with a fixed, God-oriented worldview. They thus contributed in concrete ways to the project of imagining a differently ordered world—which I earlier noted was at once compelling and terrifying for early drama theorists—by bringing a range of spectators together to encounter both new and familiar stories in a common time and place. (This spatial re-orientation is part of what Joanne Tompkins calls theatre's "heterotopic" potential, something we will explore in more detail at the end of this section.) How spectators entered the theatre space in Shakespeare's day would have had an important effect on their re-orientation, preparing them for similar kinds of potential re-orderings soon to appear on stage.

As we leave the courtyard, tickets in hand, we enter the reproduction Globe's performance space one of two ways. Groundlings enter through doors leading directly into the yard; once out of the access corridor just behind those doors, the yard and stage open up, wide and bright, before them. Once inside the yard, a groundling's orientation is largely upward: at the looming, elevated stage ahead as well as at the banks of packed gallery spectators looking down on them from above. In early modern England, the groundlings were those with the least money to spend on tickets; they would have looked literally up to, and been looked down upon by, those who could pay more (as well as those, often, with greater social status). While this orientation of bodies in space reinforces social hierarchy in key ways, it's worth noting that it is not entirely the same social hierarchy typical of a royal Renaissance theatre, which, as Carlson notes, would have been arranged visually and spatially so that the best seats in the house had an unobstructed view of the monarch, with those of highest rank seated around him or her, their proximity to the monarch dictated directly by relative royal status and hierarchy (1989: 140, 142). Instead, at English commercial theatres like the Globe, spatial privilege was (and is) granted to those with money—heralding the beginning of modern capitalism, and the parallel shift away from bloodline as the most important determinant of status and wealth.

Shakespeare's groundlings were not just looking up at their so-called superiors; they were also looking up at the stage, on which, in plays like *As You Like It* or *All's Well That Ends Well*, they could witness characters in disguise climbing the social ladder or outwitting those of the opposite gender to effect positive material change in their own lives. They were looking up at actors who were also entrepreneurs, or even stars; young men in the groundling audience watched young boys who were apprentice workers, stars-to-be. In other words, groundlings were looking up at a version of themselves, men (and women, at least in the fiction) of an emerging middle class. And the male actors on stage were looking out at them, too.

Shakespeare's tragedies and comedies rarely conform to the unities of time and place that Aristotle's neoclassical followers insisted upon, nor to their project of encouraging theatrical realities to follow existing social orders; instead, the plays take spectators across the seas, from one battlefield to another, or from palace to forest of Arden in a single three-hour window. Players appeal to audience members directly—both to those in the pit (where you might get roped into the action!) and, with arms wide, to those in the galleries—acknowledging both the sheer numbers of spectators in front of them and the influence those spectators, never quiet and never still (especially not if they are standing!), can have on the events on stage. The "O" of the space, placing actors and spectators into constant, creative circulation, thus operated (still operates) as a means for reciprocal human imagination and invention; it requires we use not only our eyes, but also our ears, our voices, and our whole bodies to activate the show.

What of the people in the galleries, those not standing? Those with assigned seats, then and now, will enter the Globe via one of several narrow stairwells, curling tightly upwards; they will squeeze past fellow seat-holders to perch on covered wooden benches looking down on the stage. Just as for the groundlings as they enter the yard, emerging from the claustrophobic stairwells into the galleries creates for these spectators the effect of an immediate opening up and *opening out*: onto the world of the stage, and onto the pit populated by masses of people. (Today, being a groundling is a sought-after experience, though still very cheap.) For each group of patrons, then—groundling and gallery-goer, early moderns and us today—the journey into the Globe theatre is a journey into a place marked as very different from the ordinary street we've just left (or the modern building we've just exited). The vantage, from above or below, is meant to surprise and delight: suddenly we are faced not only with the vastness of the Globe stage, but also, tangibly, with the unmistakable physical proximity—the shared, embodied investment in the performance—of one another.

The Globe of Shakespeare's day offered audience members an opportunity to encounter worlds they could never physically see, histories they could not personally witness. It taught that history to some; it opened up alternative living and working possibilities to others. It operated as an imperfect yet democratic space, a public sphere in which players would be held accountable for their stories and actions by a crowd that vastly outnumbered, and literally surrounded, them. For us today, it offers a not dissimilar re-orientation. The Globe is an unmistakably communal space in a world where, thanks to the dominance of both political liberalism and digital technologies, we are often encouraged to think as individuals, accounting only for ourselves. In its late modern iteration, the Globe puts significant pressure on Western perceptions around personal space: here, it's difficult to avoid touching your fellow spectators. Contemporary audience members at the Globe are always very much aware of the space their bodies take up, of how their bodies feel in relation to other bodies packed tightly around them, and of the kinds of effects a mass of bodies in one space can have on the "official" events that take place in that space—as our applause, cheers, or jeers impact the players in front of us. The Globe, then as now, is a lesson in shared human spacing, a way of orienting us toward space as collectively embodied: made, and re-made, together.

Realism as a Spatial Art: Henry S. Turner's "Topographic" Stage

Fast-forward to the nineteenth century; it has now been over 200 years since Descartes' theories of human potential began to turn Europe away from God and monarch, effecting a profound cultural shift. As R. Darren Gobert showed us earlier, one of the effects of Cartesian thinking was architectural: the world, increasingly, was framed as a picture, and the trajectory between auditorium and stage became increasingly visually oriented. Although Cartesian thinking was revolutionary in many ways as it ushered in the Enlightenment and hurried Europe toward modernism, it also bore quite conservative side effects. For example, Marvin Carlson reveals that the same "perspectival" theatres orienting audience members visually toward the stage, and away from the embodied experience of spectatorship common at older public theatres like the Globe, also featured more prominent social stratification than ever before. Royal or aristocratic visitors had private boxes with separate entrances, ensuring that "everyone [could] attend the theatre according to his rank and means and [...] gather there with his usual social companions" (Pierre Patte, qtd. in Carlson 1989: 142). As the mix of publics at the theatre grew more and more heterogeneous through the early nineteenth century, separate entrances, lobbies, and bars ensured that "there was little or no actual overlapping of social spaces," even when all visitors to the theatre ultimately sat and watched the same performance in the very same auditorium (149).

These are the kinds of theatre buildings that come to mind first for me when I think about the plays of Ibsen, Strindberg, and Chekhov. Big-name, "bankable" modern playwrights are featured regularly in mainstream, marquee venues in major theatre districts in cities like London, Chicago, New York, or Toronto, and these venues often feature the architectural grandeur of nineteenth-century proscenium arch spaces. But playwrights like Ibsen et al—which we now associate with "mainstream" or Broadway realism—were actually avant-garde artists in their moment, and their earliest experimental work in the then-radical naturalist style was first showcased in small, intimate theatres (such as André Antoine's famous Théâtre Libre in Paris, August Strindberg's Intima Teater in Stockholm,[9] or the Moscow Art Theatre where Stanislavsky directed). These venues featured the same forward-facing orientations and focus on sightlines as many of the larger theatres of their time, but in these smaller spaces this orientation functioned principally to pull spectators physically closer to the stage, and intellectually and emotionally *into* the carefully crafted room(s) portrayed *on* that stage. The physical shape of the auditorium, tiny and tight and forward-driving, was meant to encourage audiences to engage deeply with the "real" places and lives represented on stage. In turn, playwrights and directors offered scripts and acting practices that loaded those spaces with intense symbolic value and crowded the playing space with objects designed to materialize a known world in front of audiences.

Turn-of-the-(twentieth)-century realism, characterized by the "fourth wall" and the closed, often stifling, drawing-room world of life-like, naturalist detail, offers us one of the best examples in modern dramatic history of the "topographic" play. Henry S. Turner coins the term "the topographic stage" in his wide-ranging 2006 book, *The English Renaissance Stage: Geometry, Poetics, and the Practical Spatial Arts, 1580–1630.*[10] Writing about the turn of the sixteenth century in London, Turner notes the speed with which the city was urbanizing, and the pressures that urbanization created in an increasingly crowded, diverse, often chaotic place. London was *becoming* a city at this moment in time; everyone living and working and passing through it would therefore have needed to negotiate not only the challenges of sharing dense urban space (something that, to us today, might seem common enough), but also the challenges of coming to grips with *the very idea* of a growing, global metropolis—a spatial phenomenon altogether new in 1600 (187).

For Turner, the public stage played a central role in these daily spatial negotiations. It represented the city's changing shape directly to playgoers, and it conveyed important spatial knowledge to those playgoers—about what urban space looked and sounded and felt like, about how it was organized, and about where different people, things, and ideas fit into it. Turner explains:

> The "city" plays produced by [playwrights like Thomas Dekker, Ben Jonson, and Thomas Middleton] provided [their] spectators with a reproduction in miniature of specific, identifiable elements in the streets around them, in this way functioning as an objective screen for the processes of identification through which viewers recognized themselves as part of the collective civic entity, correlating a concept of citizenship not simply with a sense of legal and institutional belonging but with physical placement in a realistic urban topography. ... Workshops, alehouses, prisons, and private residences: all emerge as structuring

> principles for representational action in English comedy because these were the very sites in which the conflicts and fantasies of everyday urban life were taking place. (2006: 194–5)

At the turn of the twentieth century, Europe and North America were experiencing once more the kinds of social upheavals Turner explores in relation to Renaissance London: colonial expansion, rapid urbanization, technological change including significantly increased mechanization, class changes, and the ideological shifts that tend to accompany them (see Singer 2001: 17–36). Avant-garde realism incorporates, dramatizes, processes, and responds to these shifts just as Turner sees City comedy offering early Londoners a means to map, spatially, their new social realities around 1600. Realism does this by locating its conflict and tension physically inside the private family home, and often in just one or two rooms inside that home. The precise, iconic, naturalist detail—the props and decorations—of this claustrophobic setting does important spatial work here. Modernist realism puts unabashedly sacrosanct private space, and the often-hidden, often unpleasant details of the private lives that space shelters, front and center on its stage in order to question the distinctions between private and public spaces, male and female bodies, and upper- and lower-class citizens that had hitherto organized the world physically as well as imaginatively. The realist drama asks: Can these distinctions hold in this new, modern time? If so, at what cost?

Realism as Embodied Space: Stanton Garner and Theatrical Phenomenology

Avant-garde modern realism, as I am using the term here, is intimately related to naturalism. (I will clarify further the distinction between realism and naturalism below.) Theorists of modern drama understand naturalist space to be intensely intimate, subjective, almost fetishistic in its focus on material details on the one hand, and deeply symbolic, framed objectively for analysis, ideologically and politically loaded on the other. The apparent contradiction between these two frameworks for reading naturalist space—subjective yet also objective; materialistic yet also symbolic; private yet also political—in fact drives theories of how avant-garde realism does its political work. In his groundbreaking 1994 book, *Bodied Spaces: Phenomenology and Performance in Contemporary Drama*, Stanton B. Garner, Jr. uses phenomenology—a philosophy of perception derived from Edmund Husserl, Martin Heidegger, Maurice Merleau-Ponty, and Gaston Bachelard, among others—in order to explore the ways in which drama after 1950, both naturalist and non-naturalist, refocuses theatre away from the Cartesian picture-frame of the Enlightenment period and toward a "plastic" (55), fully embodied theatre with a complex and often contradictory relationship to the stage-as-image.

"Bodied spatiality is at the heart of dramatic presentation," Garner writes in his introduction, "for it is through the actor's corporeal presence under the spectator's gaze that the dramatic text actualizes itself in the field of performance" (1). In other words, Garner argues that the theatre is a cultural zone in which we can fully appreciate "space" as *made up of* human bodies and their interactions, not pre-given to house them nor merely decorated by them. (In this way, Garner's approach to stage space is very similar to Lefebvre's approach to social space; notably, both are influenced by phenomenology.[11]) Until the second half of the nineteenth century, painted curtains on proscenium stages framed actors performing stock gestures; their words, bodies, and physical language served the story, were tools of narrative, and the painted backdrop was no more than a backdrop. In a world mechanizing and urbanizing "at full throttle" (Singer 2001), though, the human body and its shifting place in social space once more took on radical signification; thus, the theatre's project at the end of the nineteenth century involved politicizing the modern human body by revealing it in its material, environmental, and intersubjective—i.e., its socio-spatial—complexity.

The goal of all phenomenological inquiry is to "redirect attention from the world as it is conceived by the abstracting, 'scientific' gaze (the objective world) to the world as it appears or discloses itself to the perceiving subject (the phenomenal world)" (Garner 1994: 2). A phenomenology of theatre attempts, in other words, to return the physical, material body to the visually oriented theatre in a thorough-going way. Just as the seventeenth-century shift to Cartesianism and the picture-frame was ultimately a spatial move designed to locate human consciousness (and the human eye) at the center of a new world order, so is phenomenology a spatial methodology that seeks to account for the body as a subject in (and of) social space. As Garner notes, the "field of performance" is always both "scenic space"—"given as spectacle to be processed and consumed by the perceiving eye, objectified as field of vision for a spectator who aspires to the detachment inherent in the perceptual act"—and "environmental space," "'subjectified' (and intersubjectified) by the physical actors who body forth the space they inhabit" (3). While historical theatres have always been shaped to greater or lesser degrees by this dual sense of theatrical spacing, at the turn of the twentieth century the tension *between* space as "scenic" or pictorial and space as "environmental" or embodied became a central aspect of realism, key to its topographical work. The avant-garde realist theatre emerges, Garner's book argues, in order to reckon with the spaces inhabited, and activated, by the human body in the industrializing, modern world.[12]

Naturalist theatre practitioners are distinguished from other realist artists by their commitment to what is sometimes called "environmental determinism," or the notion that human beings are shaped entirely by environmental factors (social, biological, economic, and genetic, among others). While environmental determinism can be helpfully aligned with cultural materialism in some ways, it also undergirds naturalism's scientific focus. Naturalism sought to create objective viewpoints from which spectators might observe and ultimately diagnose the characters on stage as products of their environments, as though audience members were doctors and the characters their patients (see Diamond 1997, esp. "Realism's Hysteria"; Garner 2008). However, as Garner points out, if the "abstracting, 'scientific' gaze" of an "objectified" worldview (1994: 2) is encouraged at the intimate, detail-oriented, avant-garde realist theatre, the bearer of that gaze also inevitably confronts and becomes entangled with the "perceiving subject" and the "phenomenal world"—precisely because naturalism places bodies both on and off stage in close proximity to each other and to the material objects making up their shared, "real" world beyond the theatre (88–90). This paradox—cool, detached, objective; yet also messy, crowded, intersubjective—is one of many seeming contradictions that makes naturalism an ultimately ethical genre for theorists like Kirk Williams (2006) and Elin Diamond (1997), one ideally suited to the work of exploring the contradictory phenomena impacting the human body under late modernity.

For Garner, objects play a central role in this aspect of naturalism's work. Making the stage seem as real as possible inevitably meant crowding it with masses of "real" stuff (91); the body on stage could then become "a site of agency *within a field of things*" (1994: 88, my emphasis), determined by a field of relationships mediated by things. Props allow characters to act upon them and to be acted upon in turn; the weave among character, object, and space in naturalist drama shapes narrative meaning and its social and political reverberations. Think, for example, of Hedda Gabler's richly symbolic pistols, inherited from her father. They structure the space of the stage as they sit nestled below the governing picture of her father at the heart of Ibsen's scenic design. They shape Hedda's relationships to Eilert Løvborg, Judge Brack, and her husband, as she uses them to wield "soft power" over the play's men, knowing that such is now the limit of her influence as a newly married, middle-class woman. As she holds a pistol in her hands and aims it through the garden door, she seeks to project herself beyond the house in which she now feels trapped; her hand on the trigger of the gun represents the tension between her desire to be so much more than her married woman's (pregnant) body can be, and the limits placed upon that body by the rules of gender, class, and decorum structuring her society. Finally, the pistols allow her to control—in a limited and limiting way, and yet still—the ending to her story, as she shoots herself behind a stage curtain, in the inner chamber of the set, in the deepest, most private, least visually accessible space on stage.

As a proto-feminist character in a naturalist drama, Hedda Gabler takes shape as a body in Lefebvrian social space, a body whose wide-ranging sense of self competes with the socially determined spaces and objects that encase it. Garner explains that props always "ground the individual, *as body*, in its material surroundings" (1994: 90, my emphasis), and, as Elin Diamond notes in "Realism's Hysteria," her analysis of the play in relationship to Freud's *Studies in Hysteria* (1997), Ibsen's text embeds precise clues for both actors and readers, inviting us all to regard Hedda as radically *of her body*, burdened with materiality in the form of her growing pregnancy. Performers like Elizabeth Robins, who pioneered the role of Hedda in London at the turn of the twentieth century, looked to these clues to ground the character in a tell-tale, pathological physicality: her expressions, her gestures, her physical make-up all cued spectators to Hedda's toxic relationship with both her body and her material surroundings. Audience members would therefore have been invited to read simultaneously the story Hedda's body revealed about her, the story her love of some objects (the pistols) and hatred of others (Aunt Tesman's flowers, the new house) revealed about her, *as well as* the stories she tries to tell about herself. Meaning—Hedda's "truths"—emerges only when we examine the tensions among these competing narratives, played out across body, object, and space.

Acting in Lived Spaces: Konstantin Stanislavsky's "System"

Naturalism, paradoxically, contracts stage and auditorium space almost claustrophobically, ramming it with bodies and stuff, and upping the tension thereby—even as it demands our cool, objective distance from the worlds it presents in such perfect detail. As it does this, it lifts our relationships to modern space and to the other bodies in that space up for debate. Not only plots and playwrights, stage directions and well-dressed sets support this work, though; changes in acting practice at the turn of the twentieth century were also key to the ways avant-garde realism and naturalism charged space politically at the theatre.

Konstantin Stanislavsky is famously associated with a particular brand of "emotional realist" acting: the idea of "living a character" or mining one's own emotional history for stage fodder. (The latter is a practice that is actually attributable to Lee Strasberg, not Stanislavsky; the Method and the System are related, but not the same.) In fact, Stanislavsky was at best a reluctant realist; he did not use the term "naturalism" to describe his work, and he was not interested in creating an acting method for any single genre. Rather, he was driven by a commitment to "truthful" embodiment, and by a firm belief in the connection between physical action and emotional creation—i.e., in the performing arts as embodied, spatial arts.

As Sharon Carnicke's 1998 book *Stanislavsky in Focus* reveals, Stanislavsky's "system" centers on the all-important concept of "experiencing" (123). "Experiencing" empowers actors as co-creators rather than consigning them to the role of textual interpreters; it also offers actors a kind of doubled lens through which to view and evaluate their work by taking stock moment-to-moment of how the labor of living in and through a role *feels* (108–9). In his lessons for students (compiled in new, more accurate translations by Jean Benedetti in *An Actor's Work*, 2008), Stanislavsky constantly encourages trainee actors to observe carefully the world around them, and to abandon stock gestures that "point to" emotion (say, a hand to the forehead for "woe!"). Instead, he argues, actors should work organically through lived action, from which genuine feeling may emerge. This move is entirely phenomenological: it makes space—the worlds in which actors live; the rehearsal rooms where they train; the stages on which they perform—a full collaborator in modern acting practice. Rather than produce the image of a feeling, Stanislavsky wants actors to learn to produce lived feeling by operating as agents "in a field of things" (Garner 1994: 88)—by using lived space and felt objects as co-creators, along with fellow performers.

One of the assumptions performance theory has long held about emotional realist acting practice is that it collapses the space between an actor's body and that of a character, erasing the differences between them (Diamond 1997: 52). Carnicke's analysis of "experiencing," however, reveals that Stanislavsky's system may also be understood as a *space-making* practice designed to return lived bodies to the worlds around them, producing character through studied embodiment grounded in phenomenal observation. Consider, for example, the episode in *An Actor's Work* when Tortsov (Stanislavsky's persona in the text) invites the students Kostya and Vanya onto the rehearsal stage in order to play the scene he calls "burning money" (Stanislavsky 2008: 160–4). Kostya asks for prop money to burn, but Tortsov tells him he does not need it; he asks Kostya to use his imagination instead—to remember what touching, counting, holding money feels like, and to discover through that remembrance the missing object in his hands. Kostya attempts to perform "counting" the money through mime but does so unconvincingly; Tortsov stops him almost immediately. Tortsov then guides Kostya step-by-step through the small details that often go unnoticed when we touch, use, and exchange objects (like paper money) in our everyday lives. Through this physicalization process, Kostya finds he can materialize paper roubles where there are none:

> As a result of all the logical actions Torstov suggested to me I developed a new attitude towards working with "nothing." It exactly filled the role of the imaginary money, or rather, enabled me to focus on an object which in reality did not exist. They are not the same thing at all, waving one's fingers meaninglessly and counting the dirty, used rouble notes which, in my mind, I was looking at. As soon as I felt the truth of physical action I felt at home on the stage. (2008: 161)

In this example, Kostya's labor exemplifies "experiencing": he uses his embodied memory of objects in the world to produce, on stage, the physical sensations of counting money, rendering the image of his actions believable (maybe even *perceptible*) to observers. He transforms thin air—the spaces around his body, the space his actions take up—into "the real world," into recognizable, everyday phenomena. His character in this moment does not erase his lived body; his lived embodiment instead produces character as a function of shared, actionable space.

The "burning money" episode, along with many others in *An Actor's Work*, demonstrates that Stanislavsky's "emotional realism" is a rigorous, creative, materially and critically aware form of physical and psychosocial work, one that encourages actors to operate self-reflexively and to maintain a level of critical distance in a role, even when they appear to be doing the opposite. "Living" a role means inhabiting two bodies at once: one's lived, human actor's body, and the body that intensive character work produces through and alongside it. This layering builds a phenomenological empathy, as well as a level of critical distance, into realist acting practice, making space between acting body and fictional body, and potentially exploiting the tensions between them in order to mobilize a politics, or spark debate (see Tom Hiddleston speaking in Cheek by Jowl 2008, 3:56-4:45). It is this exact potential that Bertolt Brecht used for his own very different (political) ends as he built his theory of "epic" realism in the 1930s and 1940s, in which actors stood overtly apart from their characters and invited audiences to explore the ideological differences lying in the spaces between them.

Una Chaudhuri and "Geopathology"

"As soon as I felt the truth of physical action I felt at home on the stage": Kostya's comment reveals the extent to which the material focus of Stanislavskian acting can be grounding for actors, but as a reference to realist practice it is also somewhat ironic. This is because another key strand of theory about space and place in modern drama argues that this drama, again and again, represents the idea of home—of being "emplaced" and secure in a familiar, private space—as impossible. Some of the most important writing on this topic appears in Una Chaudhuri's 1995 book, *Staging Place: The Geography of Modern Drama*. In that volume, she coins the now-ubiquitous term "geopathology." Chaudhuri writes:

> Modern drama at first employs, as one of its foundational discourses, a … culturally determined symbology of home, replete with all those powerful and empowering associations to space as are organized by the notion of belonging. The dramatic discourse of home is articulated through two main principles, which structure the plot as well as the plays' accounts of subjectivity and identity: *a victimage of location* and a *heroism of departure*. The former principle defines place as the protagonist's fundamental problem, leading her or him to a recognition of the need for (if not an actual enactment of) the latter. (xii, emphasis in original)

Like Garner's phenomenological explorations of modern theatrical space, Chaudhuri's study ranges across a variety of dramatic forms and genres—including the non-realist, even anti-realist work of playwrights like Pinter, Beckett, and Shepard.[13] The roots of her study, however, lie in the topographical qualities of avant-garde realism: in its ability to represent "our world" in rich material detail to audiences, only to undercut that perfection deftly via plot and character, leaving all of us feeling oddly homeless at play's end.

The condition of geopathology is especially acute for Chaudhuri in avant-garde realism's stifling, overstuffed, private spaces like parlors, kitchens, and bedrooms; it is here that she locates what she calls the "geopathic dramaturgy" (56) of playwrights such as Eugene O'Neill, Ibsen, and their contemporaries. In these cases, the mimetically perfect comforts of the well-dressed play-space, married to characters unhappy, ungrounded, or locked into narratives of entrapment, generate a condition of uncanniness. In a 1919 essay, the psychoanalyst Sigmund Freud defined uncanniness, or *Unheimlichkeit* (literally: un-homeli-ness), as a sense of being at once in a place utterly familiar, and yet at the same time feeling not in any way "at home" in one's self, one's body, or one's world (Solga and Tompkins 2017: 79). Think back once more to Hedda, her pistols, the open garden door, and that small room at the rear of the set where she commits suicide: trapped in her home, Hedda yearns for escape. Chaudhuri invokes Ibsen directly as she articulates the core paradox of geopathology in her introduction: "Again and again ... the crisis of the concept of home appears as the collision therein of two incommensurable desires: the desire for a stable container for identity and the desire to deterritorialize the self" (1995: 8).

Using Chaudhuri's schematic, we can understand the pervasive, embodied, *felt* sense of illness and disease—and the parallel, paradoxical need for a scientific eye, for a doctor's objective gaze—at the modern realist theatre to be, in fact, *a disease of place and space*. During the dramatic global changes that accompanied industrial modernization through the end of the nineteenth and the beginning of the twentieth centuries, many spaces that were once—or at least, were imagined to be—safe, secure, and above all unchanging (like a family home, or a village where extended family could always be found) could no longer be relied upon as such. "Home" became a shifting signifier—strangely untethered to singular bodies, spaces, or identities. Modernity "at full throttle" brought mass migration, moves from family villages to isolating cities, from farms to tenement buildings; the result was the loss of traditional home-ways, and of crucial shifts in the very idea of a "home," for many modern subjects.

For still others, those locked into traditional social patterns (women and servants, for example) despite substantial social change in the public sphere, the modern progress narrative brought new desires and disruptive questions (see Solga and Tompkins 2017: 77–80). Who owns the "castle" that is the "man's home"? Who works there, and how are they compensated? What else might they want to do with their days? Who are these new people sharing our neighborhoods, our cities? What do they look and sound and smell like, and can we assimilate their different, dissonant bodies into our senses of "self" and "home"? Home as both physical place *and* imagined horizon comes under minute scrutiny in modern, avant-garde realism as the genre crafts a poetics of the modern human body grounded—ironically, and once more paradoxically—in always-changing physical, social, public and private spaces. As Chaudhuri argues throughout *Staging Place*, modern theatre, and in particular avant-garde realism, weaves together the contradictory ideas of home, exile, and dispossession as it dramatizes "the experience of longing to belong, linked inherently to a powerful sense of, and even need for, exile from a suffocating home" (Solga and Tompkins 2017: 79). Uncanny in its richly detailed, mimetic places that run headlong into characters desperate to get out, away, to go somewhere else, avant-garde realism and naturalism are above all "topographic" in their offer to modern audiences of the image of a perfect home none of us may ever inhabit—and thus of a chance to reinvent entirely what it means to "belong" to a place and to the others in it. These genres let us question our own locational positions in the modern world, and they ask us to open our imaginations to different kinds of groundings, different forms of habitation shared with a range of bodies, and with a range of desires, from both "here" and "elsewhere."

Contemporary Lens #3: The Heterotopic Stage

By the middle of the twentieth century, much modern realism had been displaced by other forms of the theatrical avant-garde. Realism's claims to verisimilitude—to show the world to audiences "as it really is"—came under fire as naïve, as the postwar world woke up to the idea that reality might be fractured, highly subjective, and multiplicitous rather than singular, objective, and locatable via a glance through a proscenium arch. Although much recent work on stage realism has complicated this reading of the genre (see Barker, Solga, and Mazer 2013, for example), for avant-garde practitioners and many academics stage realism continues to represent the most traditional of theatrical spaces: a closed room placed in front of a bank of darkened viewers.

In response to realism's tight physical strictures, around the middle of the twentieth century avant-garde practitioners started leaving the theatre building proper in order to make work in the kinds of "contextual" spaces that we considered at the top of this section. This new theatrical genre is often called "environmental theatre," after the title of Richard Schechner's influential book on the form; today, its traces are most easily recognized in site-specific and immersive performance. In the final part of this section, I discuss the features of environmental theatre as well as its legacies, and link them to an important idea circulating in later-twentieth-century performance theory: that theatre can be an *active*—not merely a *representative*—agent in social justice by inviting audiences to inhabit quotidian spaces directly, to uncover some of the hidden things about those spaces that normative occupation of them masks, and thereby to enact the potential for "heterotopia" or "alternate ordering" (in Kevin Hetherington's phrase) necessary for lasting political change.

Environmental Theatre: Promises and Problems

In *Environmental Theatre* (1973), Richard Schechner writes:

> The fullness of space, the endless ways space can be transformed, articulated, animated—that is the basis

> of environmental theater design. It is also the source of environmental theater performance training. If the audience is one medium in which the performance takes place, the living space is another. The living space includes all the space in the theater, not just what is called the stage. (1–2)

As a genre of performance, environmental theatre bears a relationship to space that is starkly different from that of the avant-garde realist theatre we just explored. Rather than treating space as representational—*showing* audiences their world, reflecting it to them mimetically via prop and set, character and action, while they watch from outside the performance area—environmental theatre treats space as elastic, as fully embodied (in Garner's terms), and as undifferentiated (between acting space and viewing space). It aims to place audiences inside a performance zone that is also "lived" space, rather than in the position of objective, detached viewer of "represented" space up on the stage. Working in an environmental way means "not trying to create the illusion of a place" but instead building "a functioning space" that can be shared and used by everyone participating in the performance, not just the actors (Schechner 1973: 31).

Schechner notes that, in environmental theatre practice, what will be the final performance space evolves from the rehearsal process's "living space" via "detailed work with the performers," because "environmental design comes from daily work on the play" (11). Performers, as embodied users of lived space in rehearsal, articulate the eventual shape of the play as they explore its narrative contours; their physical actions become the architectonics of the set design. (Even then, after a show opens, Schechner explains that "the environment changes" as new aspects of the work open up and are explored by actors and spectators [11].) While audience members may or may not be invited to participate in an environmental production's action directly, they are frequently encouraged to use the space of reception non-normatively, moving around in order to change their points of view (30). As Schechner notes, this might mean they will miss some parts of the performance, while getting a deeper experience of others (6).

Environmental theatre thus actively transgresses the dividing lines between theatrical and non-theatrical space ("acting space" and "audience space"; "performing space" and "living space") that became conventional after the seventeenth-century shift to Cartesian viewing practices (driven by a singular vanishing point which organizes all perspectives on and around the stage). Actors working in an environmental mode help to shape directly where and how the larger drama will unfold. Audience members, in turn, adjust their sense of viewing privilege, coming to terms with *not* seeing or knowing everything that may happen in the performance, *not* grasping a whole, complete reality from a singular, seemingly objective viewpoint. They will be aware of their bodies as much as they will be aware of what they are seeing; they will need to move their bodies through the space in order to see "more" or "better," and in order to make choices about how, where, and what to look at (Schechner 1973: 30). Above all, "space" in this genre is not an eventual location, onto which a performance will be projected, but the very starting point for that performance, the source of its inspiration and development. Channeling the thinking of Lefebvre and Soja (and, indeed, influenced by anthropology and sociology as well as critical social theory), environmental theatre presents a theory as well as a practice of mutually constituted, socially produced spaces that are "concerned with structure and use" as much as with symbol and meaning (31). It is designed to be collaborative and fluid, as ideas and actions flow "in many directions, sustained only by the cooperation of performers and spectators" (39).

Although environmental theatre may seem a world away from realism and naturalism, it actually offers a logical extension of their spatial practices. As we've seen, realism's interest in space is topographical: it aims to reflect the lived spatial conditions of its spectators in a way that will invite them to think critically about the politics of place: where is home, who inhabits it, what do those people want or need, and which social or cultural conditions determine whether or not their needs are met. Environmental theatre shifts the method, but not the goal. Now, instead of offering an image of place to contemplate, a topography to study scientifically, it aims for active learning: a shifting ground that audiences might literally inhabit, one that might allow them to practice intersubjectivity differently while they are at a performance, and then carry that practice out into the social spaces of their larger worlds. Schechner rails against the "stupid" proscenium arch setup, complaining of its socially segregating qualities (31–3); he asks what it would mean if everyone used the same door—actors, audiences, as well as those workers hauling in the stage equipment (35). He notes that "house" is an inaccurate name for an auditorium space organized in rows rather than in more congenial groupings, and he encourages his actors, when they first enter their shared maker-space, to explore it and make it a "home" (12). His questions about the politics of lived space are, therefore, not much different from those of Ibsen or Chekhov or O'Neill. However, instead of presenting "home" as a critical topography, Schechner aims literally to enact a spatial revolution.

Schechner's influential work as both a director (of The Performance Group in New York) and a theorist defined environmental theatre for a generation of performance makers and scholars, but his work is not without problems. In *Performing Ground* (2014), Laura Levin takes the measure of Schechner's influence on twentieth-century theatre's understanding of place, especially as early environmental adopters posited their alternative to stage realism as inherently more progressive and socially equitable than older forms. Levin notes:

> While the traditional spectator is positioned outside of the stage's pictorial field, s/he is now [in environmental stagings] placed inside of the theatrical picture. ... This perception of environmental performance leads theorists to wax utopian, suggesting that it represents the absolute overcoming of the logic of world picturing. (68)

As Levin goes on to argue, however, "the total collapse of spatial difference triggered by the removal of boundaries between performance and spectator" does not necessarily break down the world-picture paradigm; rather, it often "restores the dream of spatial mastery" that theorists like Schechner attribute to traditional forms such as realism (68). How? Environmental theatre's early claims of social transformation rested on a renovation of physical performance space, but not of social relations *in* that space; the assumption was that changing a performance's spatial framework would automatically trigger a change in social relations among all participants. Lefebvre might note here that this assumption falls into the trap of the illusion of transparency; Massey would argue that it fails to recognize space as a product of social *interrelations* among those with different levels of power and agency. And indeed, using the insights of both human geography and feminist art criticism, Levin demonstrates how Schechner's spatial assumptions proved to be patently untrue.

For example, Levin explores the ways that women's bodies were frequently used—in pieces like The Performance Group's seminal *Dionysus in '69*—as a "ground" upon which male artists and spectators were encouraged to actualize a one-sided "alternative" to theatrical norms (2014: 74–5). Deployed as sexual objects, the women in Performance Group shows often found themselves framed for the pleasure of their male peers, who were able under the Group's environmental paradigm not only to look, but also to touch and encroach physically upon other bodies in sometimes uncomfortable ways. Rather than enacting a transformation of gendered social relations, Levin reveals, working "environmentally" often led practitioners to repeat certain highly normative, even destructive social patterns in theatrical spaces that looked quite different and new on the surface, but may have felt, for some performers and participants, eerily similar to the things environmental theatre claimed to resist:

> Environmental transgression, what [Arthur] Sainer calls "violating" the proscenium threshold, was literalized in the

> violation of the female body. "Getting inside the picture" registers here less as an exploration of expressive space than as incursion and conquest. ... The act of collapsing *spatial difference* reinscribes *sexual difference*, thus reinforcing perceptions of women as given to be "taken." (75, emphasis in original)

Levin's project in *Performing Ground* is not to argue against the value of "environmental performance," but to interrogate the relationship between the social and the spatial it can easily take for granted. As she examines the uptake of environmental practices in contemporary performance studies, she notes that the term is now a catch-all for any kind of performance that takes place outside of traditional theatre spaces, in which the audience participates somehow by sharing space with the spectacle rather than merely watching it (69). Levin points out here (and Harvie [2013] also notes productively) that scholars tend to assume participatory performance is inherently politically progressive, leaving the questions of *what* specific participatory performances accomplish and how, *whom* they benefit and at what costs, unspoken. In the wake of the environmental theatre "revolution," Levin argues, a more nuanced exploration of the relationship between theatrical and social spaces was urgently needed. This exploration came, in no small part, through the development of site-specific theatre practices, and their debt to the influential concept of "heterotopia."

The Heterotopic Stage: Michel Foucault and After

For most of the twentieth century, realist practices (with their traditional, proscenium arch setup) and environmental practices (with their largely undifferentiated performance and audience spaces) have existed in tandem, representing two poles on the spectrum of possible ways space can be shaped and deployed at the modern theatre. Contemporary scholars of theatrical space often engage work from across this spectrum, uncovering the local ways in which spatial innovation in a variety of theatrical frameworks may spark the possibility of social transformation beyond the theatre. One of the terms that have become important for these scholars as they chart this social potential is "heterotopia."

The term "heterotopia" comes originally from French theorist Michel Foucault. In a paper called "Of Other Spaces: Utopias and Heterotopias" (1967; English translation 1986), Foucault contrasts the theoretical perfections of imagined utopias (which, he notes, are not actual spaces we can live in, and therefore have limited political potential in the real world) with spaces that *are* lived, of our world, yet are also helpfully disruptive to our (taken-for-granted) experiences of everyday space. He writes:

> There are also, probably in every culture, in every civilization, real places—places that do exist and that are formed in the very founding of society—which are something like *counter-sites*, a kind of effectively enacted utopia in which the real sites, all the other real sites that can be found within the culture, *are simultaneously represented, contested, and inverted*. Places of this kind are outside of all places, even though it may be possible to indicate their location in reality. Because these places are absolutely different from all the sites that they reflect and speak about, I shall call them, by way of contrast to utopias, heterotopias. (3–4, my emphasis)

Important here is Foucault's use of the words "counter-sites," "represent," "contest," and "invert." While his phrasing is somewhat opaque, it is clear that Foucault understands heterotopias to be concrete, ordinary places that carry the power to represent *and also to unsettle* the meanings of other concrete, ordinary places. Heterotopias interrupt quotidian space's "given-ness"—the sense, as Lefebvre might put it, that space precedes us and our interactions within it, rather than being *constituted by* our interactions within it. They allow us to ask questions about a given space's organization, and about the social and political structures that organization (often invisibly) upholds. Heterotopias are thus a means to lay bare what Lefebvre calls space's seemingly transparent qualities—the very thing that prevents us from understanding how space functions as an agent of social and political power in our world.

As his paper progresses, Foucault names some possible heterotopias: he mentions, among other places, cemeteries, brothels, prisons, ships, and also the theatre. These kinds of sites, he argues, possess the power of a mirror: they reflect ordinary space back to us darkly, making visible to us how space shapes practices of power. Foucault also reminds us that our recognition of shared social space rests on basic acts of disavowal. Lived spaces can be conceived, seen, heard, and inhabited any number of ways; culturally, however, we often agree to look at specific places in singular ways, either through tacit mutual agreement or because a viewpoint has been shaped for us by the dominant culture in that space. When we make that tacit agreement, or submit to a dominant culture's normative spatial practice, we also agree to forget that every space holds within it the power to be seen and experienced differently—if only we might change what we choose to see of it, or whom we choose to encounter within it (and how we enact that encounter).

Speaking of the theatre in "Of Other Spaces," Foucault writes: "The heterotopia is capable of *juxtaposing in a single real place several spaces*, several sites that are in themselves incompatible. Thus it is that the theater brings onto the rectangle of the stage, one after the other, a whole series of places that are foreign to one another" (6). Two key ideas emerge from this example. First, that heterotopias juxtapose *different* spaces, thus permitting us to see spatial alternatives, "incompatible" spaces rendered together—which might in turn invite us to question their apparent incompatibility. Second, this example reveals that heterotopias invite "foreign" spaces into conversation in real time and place—in other words, that they are spaces *of difference*, or rather spaces where difference can be framed, recognized, and reckoned with. The "other spaces" of Foucault's title, then, does not simply mean "one space, and then an(other) space"—the reading we might initially imagine. Rather, it means space rendered critically, space presented "as other *to itself*."

Ghosted Spaces: Marvin Carlson, Peggy Phelan, and Alice Rayner

I find it useful that Foucault's theatrical example conjures a stage more traditional than not: he imagines "the rectangle" characteristic of the proscenium arch, not the borderless space of the performing environment. All stages, he thereby suggests, hold "space" and its uses up to our critical view—realism, with its uncannily detailed "living" rooms on stage, carries the same potential for defamiliarizing lived space as environmental theatre does. Foucault recognizes that theatrical space is palimpsestic, a series of layers. It carries with it the resonances of multiple places and times—be those within a single play world, across the shared worlds of stage and auditorium, or across multiple productions set in different places on the same stage over time. This layered quality of stage space is also one of the prompts behind contemporary performance theories of ghosting, which argue that all theatre spaces are "haunted" by past activities—dramaturgical, practical, and spectatorial—and that the ghostly nature of the stage is central to theatre's status as a cultural activity with political force.

In *The Haunted Stage*, his 2001 monograph about this phenomenon, Marvin Carlson argues that "this sense of something coming back in the theatre" is common everywhere and across all genres, because "the relationships between theatre and cultural memory are deep and complex" (2). Present experiences at a show are "always ghosted by previous experiences" (2) we may have had of the same play, or of a different play staged in the same place; scripts change only modestly from iteration to iteration, and "every physical element of the production can be and often is used over and over again in subsequent productions" (8). These practical considerations allow audiences "to bring memories of previous uses to new productions" unconsciously—or even consciously, in the form of delight in recognition (8). Carlson's is a pragmatic and helpfully straightforward "hauntology" of theatre, a history of performing made manifest spectrally in the present; the phenomenon has also, however, been given more complex theoretical shape by writers such as Joseph Roach (1996), Peggy Phelan (1993, 1997), Alice Rayner (2006), and Rebecca Schneider (2011).

In *Unmarked: The Politics of Performance* (1993), Peggy Phelan uses Lacanian psychoanalysis to develop the argument that all theatre disappears, its "live" quality contingent on its basic ephemerality. Founded in this inevitable disappearance after a live staging ends, theatre and performance become for Phelan a means to recognize and ethically represent things that were not visible in social space in the first place, what she calls the "unmarked." (Consider, for example, the impetus behind the Black Lives Matter movement—which deliberately marks *as such* lives that are frequently regarded as "less than"—or the political work, often using sophisticated performance practices, of those who strive to call attention to the "disappearances" that characterize repressive regimes [see Taylor 1997].) Phelan's enormously influential argument about liveness and disappearance at the theatre has now been problematized extensively, but its impact on performance theory remains unassailable.

In *Ghosts: Death's Double and the Phenomena of Theatre* (2006), Alice Rayner builds on the ground laid by Phelan, focusing on the "double" that is central to all mimesis: theatre is born when a "real" thing is reproduced on stage, in front of audiences who can recognize that model-copy relationship as the key to the work they are observing. Importantly, this formula holds even when the theatrical event we attend is not strictly mimetic. As soon as a performer takes a stage, that performer becomes their own double, self-plus-character; pleasure, meaning, and often political force emerge from our recognition of both figures sharing the same place and time at once. Noting the "uncanny" quality the theatrical double always produces, Rayner points to its political potential:

> To whatever extent stagecraft may be said to create mere effects and illusions, it relies on a premise that clearly divides the world into oppositions of true and false, real and unreal, visible and invisible. Theatre in its dense practices thoroughly confounds that premise on a principle of negativity or invisibility within visibility. The double in this sense is not a reflection or imitation of an original but an appearance of a dynamic contradiction. (xi–xii)

Phelan's prequel to this story in *Unmarked* argues for several ways theatre and performance can make invisibility manifest; she notes, significantly, that the challenge is *not* to make unseen things visible at last, but instead to help audience members recognize how their vision is selective, how the foregrounding of one set of things (e.g., one set of social relations in a given space) makes another set of things (different kinds of social relations, in a different ordering of that same space) disappear from the frame. (This is what Rayner means by "a principle of negativity or invisibility within visibility.")

Here, both Phelan and Rayner come into profitable collision with Foucault's notion of heterotopia. Remember that a heterotopia is defined by its capacity to bring the spaces we recognize and the spaces we *cannot or choose not* to recognize into the same reality at one time, offering us a fresh view on how we see, act upon, and live in the world, as well as fresh alternatives for ordering that world in more socially just ways. Most theoretical readings of ghosting at the theatre are at least in part concerned with space in exactly this way: Carlson and Rayner each consider props, for example, as central to the sociopolitical labor of theatrical doubling, and

Carlson devotes a chapter to the auditorium as haunted space. Schneider's *Performing Remains* and Roach's *Cities of the Dead* fold space into their hauntologies more thoroughly, as they consider performative reenactments that bring historical spaces and bodily practices into performative conversation with present-day bodies and spaces. Theatre's ghostly epistemology, they reveal, has an essential affinity with its potential to be heterotopic, revealing multiple iterations of lived space across time, and inviting their critical, dialectical encounter.

Site-Specific Theatre: Heterotopic Possibilities

Foucault argues that all theatre bears heterotopic potential; Joanne Tompkins (2014) reminds us that this potential can only be fully realized under specific circumstances. Over the last several decades, site-specific theatre has emerged as one genre that takes this potential seriously and makes it central to its labor and goals.

In her introduction to her and Anna Birch's 2012 volume, *Performing Site-Specific Theatre: Politics, Place, Practice*, Tompkins quotes an influential definition of site-specific theatre by Mike Pearson and Michael Shanks (2001):

> Site-specific performances are conceived for, mounted within and conditioned by the particulars of found spaces, existing social situations or locations ... They rely, for their conception and their interpretation, upon the complex coexistence, superimposition and interpenetration of a number of narratives and architectures, historical and contemporary, of two basic orders: that which is of the site, its fixtures and fittings, and that which is brought to the site, the performance and its scenography. (Tompkins 2012: 2)

If we unpack this dense definition we can discover the key elements of site-specific work that bring theatre's latent heterotopic potential very much into the foreground. First, Pearson and Shanks note that site-specific work is made "for," "within," and "by" the "particulars" of the spaces that shape it: performance and site are fully interrelated and "interpenetrated." "Site" here might be defined as a performance space that is in no way incidental: it is not just a display space, not just a creation-plus-display space, but a fully constitutive part of the performance, one that helps determine the final shape of the work (just as the labor of making and presenting that work impacts and changes the site in turn). This notion of performance and space as mutually constitutive is an extension, but also a complication, of Schechner's early conception of "environment"; Pearson and Shanks are careful to note that both "site" and "performance" are made up of "a number of narratives and architectures," encompassing the physical aspects of each, the social relations shaped by each, and the historical changes to these things over time—among other factors. As Tompkins aptly puts it, "studying site requires an understanding of politics and social production" local to that site, and engaging site performatively "must accommodate different aspects of place and space through time" (2012: 5). Site-specific performance is therefore, at its best, a fulsome, self-aware representation of Massey's core argument, building on both Lefebvre and Soja, that space is not just a social product, but a product of complex social *interrelations*.

The (inter)relational quality of "site"-based theatre and performance brings us to another essential element of this work: its capacity to produce tensions and uncover ambiguities. While resonances between location and content define site-specific work, the purpose of that work is rarely just to make a show in a location that mirrors its themes (and is therefore kind of cool). Pearson and Shanks claim above that the "coexistence" of site and work is "complex"; they mean that most producers of site-specific work begin by thinking heterotopically (whether or not they use Foucault's term), wondering how to "trouble" the relationship between chosen site and intended performance (Kaye 2000: 11) in order to provoke questions about invisible aspects of that site and the social relationships shaping it. The "site" in site-specific theatre isn't about physical space, then, so much as it is about process. Journeying through such a space—through its histories, investigating its role in shaping social relations in a specific place over time—as either an artist or an audience member means being prepared to shift our shared sense of "space" and "place" from fixed and location bound to social, economic, cultural, and changeable (Pearson 2010: 11). Site-specific theatre invests the relationships among performance, spectator, site, and the extra-theatrical worlds in which each is embedded with the power of critical reflection about *how* space does cultural work, how it orients and impacts our individual bodies and experiences every day—and how it might be configured differently. As Tompkins notes, "[it] is through the 'practice' of site-specific performance that such interrogation of the control [wielded by] spatiality is possible" (Tompkins 2012: 7).

As it digs into the history and contexts of a given site in order to make work *with* that site for contemporary audiences themselves embedded in an array of social and political spaces that do not always reveal their invisible power structures, site-specific theatre deliberately foregrounds a site's (and, often, an audience's) ghosts. And indeed, discourses of ghosting have been important to the way site-specific theatre and performance practitioners and scholars talk about this work. In his 2010 primer on the genre, Mike Pearson quotes Wrights and Sites artist Cathy Turner: "each occupation, or traversal, or transgression of space [by the performance/performer] offers a reinterpretation of it, even a rewriting"; Turner refers to this "occupation" as a "ghost" (10). In Birch and Tompkins' volume, Pearson explains that, for him as for Turner, "site" is the "host" and "performance" its "ghost"—that which activates site critically via its spectral, temporary presence there (Pearson 2012: 70).

This binary relationship (site as host/performance as ghost) is provisionally useful for understanding how a performance made in conjunction with a site might provoke our thinking about that site in new ways, but it lacks nuance because it positions only one half of that binary—the performance—as an agent in meaning-making. Sophie Nield offers an alternative framework for reading the ghosting powers of site-specific theatre as she traces three public performances (one royal entry and two instances of public protest) in Whitehall, London, at three different moments in history (1887, 2003, and 2010). Looking back to Phelan's theory of performance's ephemerality, she writes:

> Within the host/ghost interpretive model, there is a troubling temporal hierarchization: the site precedes the performance, which is fleeting, evanescent, almost mystical. It is present for a short time and then it is gone, leaving the site deserted and abandoned ... Demonstrations and occupations are often dismissed for precisely their time-limitation and described as temporary "tactics" in the face of a dominating and dominant power which controls and determines space. The host/ghost framework cannot help but contain the assumption that the performance disappears at the end of the "haunting" of its temporary site. (Nield 2012: 222–3)

In contrast to the above framework, Nield proposes "a differently configured relationship between site and event" that she calls (after Lefebvre, on whom she draws heavily) "a 'horizon of meaning'" (223). The horizon of meaning model argues that, as performance and site collaborate to generate a site-specific work, performance is shaped by the contingencies of the site, while site is changed *perceptually* (which, in a phenomenological reading, also means materially) through the work of performance. In this dialectical interaction, a range of new meanings may emerge, enabling the site's normally unmarked social scaffolding to appear, and to appear as provisional rather than firm and fixed (227). Reading the kettling of student protesters on Whitehall in 2010, for example, Nield explains how the heavy-handed police tactics deployed upon peaceful marchers were designed to spark anger, violence, and further police action; the kettle "performance" created the image of a firmly-in-control government on the Whitehall "site," one that attempted to counter the competing image of that government's large-scale loss of democratic support that emerged from the protesters' performative occupation of the street.

We might now glance back at the theories of ghosting we considered a moment ago and note that Nield is proposing a move from Carlson, Turner, and Pearson's pragmatic hauntology—in which theatre or site is understood as a space of traces and echoes—toward the more theoretically rich "doubleness" proposed by Rayner. In the latter framework, theatre's "otherness to itself" becomes a model for social and political relations in space, a way to make Foucault's heterotopic notion of space-as-other take shape in real place and time. Reading site-specific protest performance in one very politically loaded location (the seat of both government and royal power in Britain) across shifting historical contexts, Nield examines how such performance activates contradictory versions of Whitehall and thereby reveals for our consideration "the real tension at the heart of site" lodged in the "debates, conflicts, and struggles staged [there] around significant political and civil questions" (2012: 231).

Siting Heterotopia at the "Traditional" Theatre: The Case of *The Unknown Island*

Site-specific work is built to interrogate the hidden significances of ordinary places, but Foucault talks about the "rectangle of the stage" when he names theatre as a possible heterotopia. Can "traditional" theatre spaces be "site-specific" in their labor? In their collection of work on the genre Birch and Tompkins gather essays that push the borders of the site-specific form (Tompkins 2012: 3), suggesting that the answer is yes. To close this section of the book, then, and as a prelude to the case studies that follow in Section Two, I will briefly explore the Gate Theatre's 2017 production of José Saramago's short story, *The Unknown Island*, which used environmental as well as immersive tactics to turn both the Gate's purpose-built stage and its position within London's social, economic, and theatrical networks into a "site" worthy of performative interrogation.

My experience of *The Unknown Island* began just before audience members were let into the small (rectangular!) performance space. A female staffer stood on the stairs above us to remind us to turn off our mobile phones, but also to ask us for money. The Gate, she noted, is a not-for-profit theatre dedicated to making work for the public good; subsidized by Arts Council funding, it relies also on donations from patrons. Without those donations, the cost of our tickets would have been more than double: she named the price, to the pound and pence. She asked us, before we left for the evening, to donate whatever we felt we could, in containers placed near the box office desk.

The staffer's invocation of the material costs of making what was already a shoestring show changed the way I regarded both the space and my fellow patrons as I entered the theatre. The entire playing area was blue, covered in a washable plastic sheeting; audience members settled on benches ranged all around the periphery, and only one chose to sit on the very small rake on the right side of the space, away from the action (he later relocated). We chatted amiably to each other, occupying the "stage," which was (as Schechner would note) fully integrated with the viewing area. When the actors entered, clad in burgundy suits and paper crowns, and began to tell Saramago's story, they spoke directly to us, moved around us, sat with us, and stood on benches beside us. The whole space, containing us all and all of our actions, was perhaps 15 feet wide by 40 feet long.

Saramago's story tells of a man and woman who choose to leave a place dominated by the fortress-like palace of a king who is reluctant to open his doors to anyone but sycophants. The man asks the king for a boat, which he finally gets through sheer perseverance (he won't leave until the king opens the door); he and the woman (the king's cleaner) then go to the seaside to fix up their new vessel. They plan to sail for an island they call "unknown," but which they are certain exists. As they prepare their boat for this journey, they share food, become close, fall asleep, and dream deeply. All of these things, and the actions they imply, the actors in the Gate's production shared with us: they fed us real olives and bread and wine, set balloon animals loose around us, and lay on the ground and on the benches before and beside us. They invited us bodily to collaborate with them in making Saramago's imaginary, hoped-for, almost-certainly real "unknown" world. They engaged us in their "play"—not just the work of "the play" but the pleasure of "playing," of inventing and pretending and then realizing new places and times together. As the show ended, the "real" value of this joyous work rushed into the space when actor Zubin Varla threw open the window at the far end of the room. The sounds of cars and wind and rustling leaves in the Notting Hill night were suddenly with us, too.

Thinking later about my experience of the blue-clad, tight little space, I realized that *The Unknown Island* turned the rectangular stage of the Gate literally into a ship—another of Foucault's heterotopias. The set design prepared us to set sail for worlds, and spatial practices, not yet known, but only after that young staffer had firmly placed the theatre into the context of London's, and Britain's, neoliberal capitalist reality here-and-now. We began in economic hierarchy, divided (invisibly) between those spectators who could afford to donate and those who needed the Gate's subsidy to be able to afford their ticket. But once inside the set, the actors joined us in playful, undifferentiated community, as they asked us to help them build a world where human creativity and imagination—not socioeconomic division—is the primary driver of community structures and cultural practices. For ninety minutes we were all in it together, getting messy in the glitter-strewn blue room, this "effectively enacted utopia" (Foucault 1986: 3)—but when the window opened and the city rushed in the production dropped us back into Notting Hill, posh and wealthy West

London, into the hierarchies and austerities governing one of the world's most unequal "global" cities (Massey 2007). Leaving the small stage-room and descending the theatre's narrow staircase to street level, I thought about the Gate as a place where the social constraints of contemporary austerity are a daily, material reality, but also as a place where we might—and in fact just did!—imagine a differently configured future, a less constricted and uneven way of inhabiting social space together, even if only temporarily. In that moment, the Gate morphed for me from "theatre" to "site"—and the next time I visit, for the next show in the season, I'll be productively haunted by that changed configuration.

SECTION TWO

Extended Case Studies

In this next section of the book, I'll put the theory we explored in the previous pages into practice. The three case studies ahead include a range of works featuring a mix of genres, including naturalism, site-specific theatre, post-dramatic theatre, and urban promenade performance. In each case, I will use a blend of theoretical approaches from Section One in order to think through the spacing practices of the work under consideration. Not every case study will use all of the theoretical approaches above, and of course different readings of these case studies might use a different blend. The goal in each case will be to demonstrate how the integration of several, sometimes disparate theoretical approaches can help us better to understand the spatial labor of a given theatre event than using one, perhaps obvious, approach alone might do.

Case Study #1: *And While London Burns*

Our first case study is an "operatic audio walk in three acts"; it is similar in structure to *Her Long Black Hair* (*HLBH*), which we briefly considered in Section One. *And While London Burns* (AWLB) was developed in 2006 by Platform, a

London-based arts and environmental justice organization; it was written and directed by John Jordan and James Marriott, with music composed by Isa Suarez, and funded by the Arts Council of England. The MP3 recording remains available for free download; participants can place it on the mobile device of their choice and do the walk anytime, as often as they wish. (They can also listen to it alone at home, or when out and about elsewhere—something that makes for a very different, but nevertheless potent, experience.)

As an audio walk, *AWLB* is designed for a solo participant; the "performance" is both in the past, at the moment of its recording, and in the present, at the moment of our listening, with participant as performer. (More on this important paradox a bit later.) The walk begins at Bank tube station in the heart of the City of London's square mile. The City is the financial center of England and of Europe, and its streets find centuries-old buildings standing cheek-by-jowl with landmark skyscrapers like the "Gherkin" and the "Walkie-Talkie," which are occupied by banking, investment, and insurance corporations as well as the advertising, marketing, and law firms that service them. *AWLB* weaves through these spaces at ground level, requiring walker-auditors to navigate a range of public and not-so-public courtyards, foyers, and passageways. Finally, it circles back to reach The Monument, built by Sir Christopher Wren to commemorate the devastating London fire of 1666, and invites participants to climb to the top and look out from above, adopting de Certeau's god's-eye view on the past, present, and future of the city of London (and of the planet) as a whole.

The audio score of *AWLB* is keyed to a detective plot, which in turn is keyed to our footfalls. Two financial sector workers have been in a romantic relationship that is now disintegrating; the man (an unnamed trader, voiced by Douglas Hodge) who narrates the story is searching for Lucy, who has not only left him but has quit the City altogether; he is also searching for a new direction for himself in the wake of her disappearance. Like Lucy, he does not want to be part, any longer, of the coming climate-change catastrophe; as a finance worker, his job (like Lucy's) is fully enmeshed with what *AWLB* (and Platform, as an organization) refer to as "the carbon web" that is wreaking environmental devastation worldwide. As we walk, the piece's audio guide (voiced by Josephine Borradaile) explains which companies occupy the spaces that surround us, how they are connected one to another, and how they all connect back, inevitably, to British Petroleum, the largest corporation in the UK and the second-largest oil company in the world (at the time of the work's creation). The walk's "plot" therefore is only superficially a love story with a detective twist; at depth, the piece is a profound excavation of environmental contamination in shared social and natural spaces. It undertakes a search for a safe, future home for all residents of London as a top-tier global city.

In our discussion of this work in our chapter on environments in *A Cultural History of Theatre in the Modern Age* (2017), Joanne Tompkins and I describe the potential significance of *AWLB* this way:

> *AWLB* telescopes the "public" view of London (gleaned from history, maps, and glossy images designed primarily for tourist and overseas-investment markets) through the much more personal act of walking its streets. This telescoping produces a double-optic map of the city that merges the domestic with the socio-political: *AWLB* argues that street-level London remains an important "home"—a shared dwelling-place for millions of human beings in urgent need of protection—even for those who do not literally reside within its borders. (92)

Within this brief description, we can already see hints of the several ways that space operates politically within *AWLB*. First, this piece asks key questions about *who* is privileged to inhabit the City, call it home, and who is marginalized by it; *AWLB* consistently requires us to think about who benefits from the current configuration of City spaces, and how those spaces might be configured differently, to different benefit. The work brings the ideas of "private" space and "public" space, "urban" space and "dwelling" space, into direct, critical contact: as we undertake the walk, using ears, eyes, sense of smell, and felt touch to navigate the cues we are given through our headphones, we must switch continuously from private, interior-oriented self to public, street-oriented self. We must be constantly and keenly aware of the difference between "public space" and "private property," lest we trespass inadvertently and be reprimanded by security officers. That navigation requires us to be attuned to the *material* conditions that shape our walking (who owns this place I've been asked to enter?), to take careful note of our *embodied* experiences, moment-to-moment (how do I feel about entering this place?), and to be constantly aware of our present experiences in relation to memory—our own memories, as well as those that crisscross shared social space.

Tompkins's and my comments in the quotation above note how the "domestic" and the "socio-political" merge in this work: the city we perceive as we walk is at once as intimate as a bedroom—it is just us and the close, friendly voices between our ears—and yet, thanks to the revelatory economics lessons the trader and guide provide as we move around, the city also becomes, over the course of the walk, tangible to us as a network of political forces shaping every aspect of our present and future lives. Here, we may perceive the piece's uncanny quality, its geopathological tendencies as it marks London as both "sick" and "home." Finally, notice the use of "double optic" in the quotation above. The term comes from Elin Diamond (2001), and it describes the way *AWLB* lifts two competing spatial realities—two views of place, private and public, from multiple perspectives and moments in time—to our view, asking us to read, from the top of Wren's monument, different possibilities for the future back into the past and present the walk has uncovered for us. In this double-optic tendency, *AWLB* ends in heterotopia.

As I explore *AWLB* below, I will tell the story of my own experience of the walk, which I undertook in February 2015. As I do so, I will deploy the **cultural materialism** of urban performance studies alongside **a performance studies approach** that combines phenomenology with an exploration of cultural memory. These will be my primary tools, and I will use them to demonstrate the work's debt to **geopathology**, as well as its commitment to **heterotopia.** *AWLB* is a site-specific piece of promenade performance, but I will also make the case for its important affinities with **realist and naturalist uses of space**—a reminder that these seemingly opposing genres often "do" space with similar political force.

The Cultural Materialist Lens: Follow the Money

I began *AWLB* not from Bank tube station, as suggested by Platform, but rather from Borough Market, across London Bridge from the start of the walk at 1 Poultry. I exited the underground one stop early to purchase a coffee from my favorite vendor and to prepare for the performance with a stroll across the river. This choice meant that I approached *AWLB* as a tourist, or as a privileged local, might approach the City.

Borough Market is a very popular tourist attraction, filled with vendors selling snacks and portable treats perfect for sightseeing fuel. It is also a microcosmic representation of gentrified London, selling luxury food products (expensive cheese, organic produce, pricy olive oils, fair-trade coffee beans) to those who live in the pricy lofts, terraces, and purpose-built flats nearby (and who may well work in the City just a short trip away). Borough Market has been a fixture of goods trading in London for over a millennium, according to the market's own website (boroughmarket.org.uk). It therefore stages a competing history of the "commodity" in London to that typical in the City today: as a tangible, consumable provision, made or raised by humans, versus the abstract financial product traded on computer screens, with which the term is now primarily associated. Nevertheless, contemporary Borough Market trades largely in tourism and minor luxuries, sharing important affinities with the City ethos. At the same time, the least wealthy of its neighbors—those who live on the poverty line in state-sponsored housing in the adjacent boroughs of Lambeth and Southwark—remain invisible on its margins.

Crossing London Bridge with my takeaway coffee, I enjoyed one of twenty-first-century London's most iconic views: St Paul's cathedral to my left, the Gherkin to my right, Tower Bridge and Canary Wharf in the middle distance. Commuters passed me on bikes, in buses, and in cars on the busy road, while to my left on the millennium pedestrian bridge linking the Tate Modern and St Paul's, scores of tourists stopped for photos of the urban vista. Below us all ran the Thames, London's biggest but by no means its only waterway; scores of now-buried streams crisscross the capital, another category of invisible inhabitant. The Thames is a working river still, but it has also been folded effortlessly into the city's tourism marketing campaigns, as well as into its campaigns to attract wealthy foreign investment. Views of the water from the tops of exorbitant properties like the Shard go for premium prices. Crossing the river, it's possible to see both its ongoing commercial labor (barges moving up and down) and its touristic qualities (sightseeing boats, the vessel that links the two Tate galleries) at once. What is harder to see is the river's ecology, its state of environmental health (or lack thereof).

I have narrated my trip to the starting point of *AWLB* in some detail in order to demonstrate how it shaped, materially as well as imaginatively, my viewpoint as I approached the performance. Just as the physical spaces of theatre façade, lobby, and auditorium shape our entry into a piece of conventional theatre, the route I took to the walk's starting point framed my perspective for the performance ahead. I was both local and tourist, both enmeshed in the labor of the City and elevated above it. As I crossed London Bridge I resided briefly in the place where London is all image, a series of world-pictures for me to enjoy, *flâneur*-like, and ultimately (like I did my coffee) to consume and toss away. Yet I also had (and would have, for the next seventy minutes) my feet firmly on pavement, other bodies and vehicles moving swiftly around me, feeling the concrete, feeling already some fatigue in my legs.

There are two other ways in which materialist analysis can support entry into *AWLB*. The first focuses on the spaces—buildings, sidewalks, businesses, tower lobbies—that surround us as we walk the City during the work, and which *AWLB* deliberately foregrounds, along with the river Thames, in its narrative and in its instructions to us. (We cannot help but encounter the materiality of the City-world here, and I'll discuss this aspect of the walk in a moment, as part of its phenomenological labor.) The second materialist approach to *AWLB*, however, focuses on the factors influencing Platform as its creator: its mandate as an organization, its funding structures, and its role within London's arts and social justice networks.

On their website's "About Us" page, Platform describe their organization like this:

> Platform is different. We combine art, activism, education and research in one organisation. This approach enables us to create unique projects driven by the need for social and ecological justice. Platform's current campaigns focus on the social, economic and environmental impacts of the global oil industry. Our pioneering education courses, exhibitions, art events and book projects promote radical new ideas that inspire change.
>
> How we work is important to us. We operate through collective decision-making. Our team includes campaigners, artists and researchers who act together and with networks to achieve long-term, systemic goals.

This description indicates that Platform is dedicated to interdisciplinary labor, collective responsibility, transparent democracy, and, importantly for a reading of *AWLB*, ecological justice. While of course a company's claims on its own social media platforms and web pages will only ever tell its version of its story, in Platform's case the comprehensiveness of its online offerings—including pages detailing publications, funding structures, and governance—implies an ethos in which no aspects of its work are intentionally hidden from public view. An extensive press archive on the Platform site (importantly, this archive contains links to independent news sources and blogs, not summaries or pull-quotes) reveals that the organization routinely gets involved with ecological justice discussions in the arts, alongside like-minded groups such as LADA, and does not wish to hide or otherwise "spin" how it is represented elsewhere.

One of the most important questions a materialist analysis of a theatre company can ask is: Where does the money come from? Platform lists its funders in a sub-menu on its "About Us" page, and it includes those who donate regularly as well as those who have made recent one-time gifts. Platform also provides a link to its ethics guidelines for fundraising, and it indicates in the footer of all of its web pages that it is "oil sponsorship free." Indeed, one of Platform's major preoccupations in the public sphere is the sponsorship by Big Oil of large cultural venues such as Tate Britain; Platform is dedicated not only to exposing environmental injustice in the global finance industry, but especially to exposing the ways in which oil and gas interests that are harming the planet may work their way as funders into arts and culture presentations that may otherwise appear value-neutral or even politically progressive. The money behind an arts event does not always determine its orientation, but it's rare that sponsors do not wish to get some tangible benefit from their donation—even (and especially) if that benefit is that they may, as an organization, thereby appear more socially conscious in the public eye. (*AWLB* makes a point of noting this about British Petroleum, too.)

Personally, I sympathize with Platform's mandate and goals; for a materialist analysis, however, that sympathy is less important than is thinking through the implications of mandate and goals, as well as funding structures, for the work Platform is making. In this case, it's clear that the subject matter of *AWLB* aligns directly with Platform's environmental justice focus. The work's dedicated website (andwhilelondonburns.com) indicates the piece was made with Arts Council funding, but it's unlikely that it did not also benefit from other of Platform's more directly environmentally focused funding dollars, such as those from Greenpeace UK. *AWLB* literally walks us through the "carbon web" blanketing the City, which we can also read about extensively on Platform's website. In this sense, we might regard *AWLB* as not simply a piece of art, but as an education tool dedicated to explicating environmental justice research undertaken by Platform, in concert with their larger organizational mandate. Again, while we may be in sympathy with this project politically, it is important for us to understand *materially* that *AWLB* is not a "neutral" piece of art (no art work is), but is rather a work tied explicitly to larger, publicly as well as privately funded, social and political goals. This information shapes *AWLB*'s orientation in space. While it invites us to travel the City at street level, its voices will consistently direct our attention both above and below: at the "carbon web" unseen in the air that links all humans, organizations, and financial interests in the City and beyond; and at the waterways we cannot any longer see below city streets, as well as at the water that—the work argues—will soon rise along with global temperatures and swallow the City whole.

Phenomenology and Cultural Memory: When Space Speaks

Arriving at 1 Poultry, I headed into a lower-ground level courtyard, where the walk begins. My view on the City, and on the performance, opened from below: in the place where water still runs unseen, in a place so built up it is hard even to notice that I am, technically, underground. This gesture is important: *AWLB* consistently aims to place participants in lived, felt relationship to the spaces we navigate together every day.

One of the key ways *AWLB* conveys its environmental justice message is by asking me to experience the almost abstract quality of City "space" as a function of the natural world it actively conceals, both in the morass of concrete towers that comprise it and in the work City firms do to disguise the environmental devastation wrought by their business practices.

Although *AWLB* is concerned, at content level, very much with the material (i.e., social and environmental, as well as economic) effects of BP and its cognate corporations, a phenomenological approach can help us unpack how it delivers this content in a way that can "land" meaningfully in participants' bodies (and minds) and activate memories individual as well as shared. As Carlson observes in her analysis of *HLBH*, pre-recorded audio walks always mobilize two lived realities at once. The first is the reality perceived (and shaped) by the artists who created the original recording, typically by walking the route during the making process and recording ambient sounds and voices to edit into the finished product. The second is the reality perceived by each individual participant who undertakes the walk at a different time, and who bears their own lived memories of its spaces with them—as Carlson bears her memories of Central Park with her on Cardiff's walk. The space *between* these two realities is activated by the audio walk, and indeed becomes the "venue" in which the walk actually "takes place." I hear and perceive the reality of the makers/narrators in my headphones, but I also, constantly, perceive the reality of my lived place and time as well. I must navigate both of these spaces simultaneously, by using the instructions I hear (turn here; cross the road there), but also by constantly adapting those instructions to match the given circumstances of this place now, perhaps years on since the recording was made. What the walk "remembers" of this place in one moment in time is not what I will remember of it; I must bear witness to both realities, and in turn they will shape my own enduring memories of the spaces I traverse.

In this way, walks like *AWLB* become exercises in complex urban embodiment. They reveal the labor quotidian urban performance always requires of us, but which it often conceals from us in its very "everyday" state. As Stanton Garner—as well as Doreen Massey—would note, an audio walk returns us to space as inherently intersubjective, embodied, relational; it demonstrates "place" to be a function of human interactions, and of human-object relations, all of which have their own expressive powers. Laura Levin would add that, in the process of activating the space between two embodied realities housed on the same site, such walks enable space *to speak to us*: that is, to raise its voice in contrast to those who would speak for or over it, and in contrast to those who would argue that "space" is simply "given" (for us to use as a tool of self-representation) rather than made manifest in our reciprocal engagements with it. In her 2009 article "Can the City Speak?" Levin argues that understanding urban space as "*communicating in a material language particular to itself*" gives us a crucial tool for understanding its social, political, and eco-critical capacity (241, emphasis in original).

A perfect example of space speaking in this way occurred for me just minutes into *AWLB*. The guide's voice invited me to take the escalator to ground level of 1 Poultry; the soprano (Deborah Stoddart, who also voices Lucy) sang, in a melancholy minor key, "look up, look up to the sky." Then the trader's voice took over; it asked me to leave the building and cross the road to the "roman ruins" opposite, the remains of the Temple of Mithras. I did as instructed—only to find a massive construction site. Few of the landmarks on the recording were there for me to grab onto; I searched and discovered at last a sign that indicated the ruins had been moved during the building of a new office complex. Over the course of my site search I detached momentarily from the recording in my ears, finding myself immersed fully in my immediate spatial circumstances. I was brought back, ferociously, to my body as "extraneous" to the spaces around me: the scaffolding made it hard to orient myself in relation to the guide's instructions, the traffic island the guide told me to use seemed to be missing, the stories the trader told in my ears bore no relation to what I was seeing, smelling, or feeling. On top of everything else cars and buses rushing past left me little safe room to retrace my steps. I felt outside the self that was hailed by the audio walk, and yet also entirely too much "of my body" to fit comfortably into the curtailed spaces left by the building project. This feeling of uncanniness—of being at once performatively out-of-place and yet reduced to my bare physical self and its most basic need (safety on the street)—made my failed encounter with the Temple of Mithras one of the most emotionally impactful parts of my *AWLB* experience.

When I got home, I investigated the building site that had had such a strong, felt impact upon me. My research revealed that the complex going up on the site of the temple was the new EU headquarters of the American finance and media giant Bloomberg. Once completed, the buildings would "house" the temple ruins, as well as an information center (the "London Mithraeum," part of "Bloomberg SPACE") that would be open to the public for educational visits. The Mithraeum website (the building and center are now complete), as we might expect, reveals none of Bloomberg's business or journalism activities. Rather, it showcases how the corporation "gives back" to London and Londoners by curating its history and making it available once more to the public. The center is free to visit, but lest we grant Bloomberg too much credit for this, it's worth noting that the temple's ruins were *always* free to visit: not only in the sense of having no admission fee, but also in the sense of not requiring visitors to enter the intimidating, private headquarters of a multinational corporation in order to do so. (The Mithraeum has a separate public entrance, but it is tricky to find, as it faces into the complex, not onto the street; when I visited in December 2017 I had to ask a doorman at the Bloomberg main entrance to help me find it.) Today, the "Mithraeum" invites us to applaud Bloomberg's philanthropy while *not* observing the company's occupation of public land and shared history, its transformation of archaeological heritage into private property, or its use of a (former) community asset as evidence of its progressive social-mindedness.

The new Bloomberg complex is massive but sympathetically designed, with modest-height towers and huge windows connecting business and pavement; at three high-traffic spots in the Bloomberg plaza an art commission, "Forgotten Streams" by the Spanish artist Cristina Iglesias, even commemorates the now-buried Walbrook River (though the information plate says nothing of the role corporate interests like Bloomberg have played in the systematic burial of London's ancient waterways). Ordinary visitors to the Mithraeum would typically have no idea about Bloomberg, its involvement in global financial markets, or its political influences (which lean moderately right); rather, their impression of the corporation would likely be colored entirely positively by its investment in the preservation of London's past, as well as by its prominent installation of a piece of ecologically minded public art. The embodied perspective granted a participant of *AWLB* moving around the site, however, allows for multiple orientations toward the site's present, its past, and its future—as home to the temple, and the trader, and Bloomberg—to appear at once. Questions emerge thanks to the tensions that arise as these several orientations collide, precipitated by the prompts the walk provides in our headphones. In 2015, as I anxiously navigated the construction site, I asked myself: Where is the temple? What is this new building? May I enter, and if so how? Where do I fit into this space, right now? These questions drove my actions, but also my curiosity; they shaped my embodied reactions, my emotional orientation toward both recording and site, provoked my later critical examination, and have defined my enduring understanding of what kinds of cultural memories adhere to the Bloomberg complex, and what kinds of cultural memories are not welcome. (Certainly, *AWLB* and my investigations into Bloomberg have now firmly shaped my personal memories of the entire Cannon Street area.)

Here, we might productively—if perhaps unexpectedly—also remember the lessons of Stanislavsky's method of physical actions, and his instructions to Kostya: Can you remember how it *feels* to hold a match, to count money? Can you hold the memory of your bodily experience in balance with the physical reality you face right now, and use it to produce a believable, "real" action in the present? During my search for the Temple of Mithras, the trader's and guide's voices on the audio recording brought me to a felt sense of being in the space directly in front of me, but *differently*. The guide reminded me, first, that I was "strolling in the shadow of Morley," a corporation that owns over 2 percent of BP's shares and is responsible for 2 percent of its impact on the globe; Morley, as I walked in February 2015, seemed still to be there. Then, the guide invited me up a small staircase, toward a small birch tree, along a railing, her footsteps echoing in what sounded like a much less busy version of the street where I was standing; the places she referenced were all gone. The memory embedded on the recording led me to a double-optic experience of the space I found myself in: my actions were conditioned both by the needs imposed by the script I heard spoken (the memory of a different embodiment, that of the script's creators), as well as by the needs of my physical "given circumstances" in the moment of listening. While of course I was not preparing a character for performance as Kostya is in Stanislavsky's text, I was, in a sense, maneuvering through the same processes of careful enactment and discovery that allow a character to develop through an actor's blend of personal and social memories and immediate, embodied encounters with space as a true collaborator in the performance process. Thus, although my encounter with Mithras was a "fail" in many respects, it also grounded me as a character in the walk's narrative, and as a public stakeholder in the larger journey of *AWLB*.

Site-Specific Realism: From Geopathology to Heterotopia

We might say my encounter with the absent temple of Mithras left me briefly homeless; I was ungrounded and untethered, fighting to get the walk back on track. While this was not planned by the creators of *AWLB*, it's certainly not out of step with the work's larger goals, not only because Bloomberg operates inside the carbon web, but also because the walk emphasizes, throughout, a feeling of being unable to get, or return, home. Here, *AWLB* connects to our exploration of geopathology in Section One, and through it to the spacing practices of modernist realism.

The trader who shapes the walk's narrative has left his office before the walk begins. He says multiple times that he needs to get back to that office—yet he never makes a move. Instead, he wanders the streets with us, occasionally suggesting this is a problem (he'll be missed, needs to collect his things, tell his friend Paul he's not returning), but increasingly he comes to terms with never going back to work. He decides to go home instead—and yet, again, he makes no move to do so. By the third act ("Water"), he turns us instead toward the Thames, where we can "really feel" the valley, London's topography showing itself "sensuous[ly]" beneath the layers of concrete (Levin 2009: 241). In this way, *AWLB* suggests that the "homes" we have come to regard as normative in the global, industrialized city—our workplaces, cubicles or small offices, or maybe just a desk or counter; our flats, our rooms, our beds—are fundamentally inadequate to our, and to our planet's, long-term needs. Choosing the valley, the river, means both choosing the natural spaces barely visible to the inhabitants of concrete, modern London, and choosing also a different future, grounded in the painful excavation of a buried and forgotten past.

Above, while discussing Garner's work on theatrical phenomenology, I wrote: "The tension *between* space as 'scenic' or pictorial, and space as 'environmental' or embodied, became a central aspect of realism, key to its topographical work" (p. 58). Starting from the ground—from underground, in fact—and literally working its way skyward, to end at the top of the Monument, *AWLB* engages directly with the environmental crisis embedded in Heidegger's "world-picture" and de Certeau's "god's-eye view." It tackles the ethical and ecological problems created by regarding space from on high, from the place where we locate ourselves as central to all forms of worldly representation, as a series of locales to be conquered or resources to be plundered for our own self-interest. As we weave through the narrow streets of the City with the trader, we find ourselves frequently in ironic orientation to the "god's-eye view" of financial London: in stunningly close, felt proximity to places designed to be gawked at from afar. There's a demystifying quality about this proximity, as though we are reaching for something marked as to-be-admired-but-not-touched, and uncovering its utterly ordinary, even banal properties, the wizard behind the curtain.

At the end of Act Two ("Dust"), for example, the guide deposited me at the base of the Gherkin, the famous pickle-shaped tower on St Mary Axe, home to Swiss Re, a massive, global re-insurance firm. Here, I learned that the Gherkin was (as of 2006) only half-occupied, and I learned that Lucy worked for Swiss Re. There are purpose-planted trees all along the approach to the building, as well as benches designed to make it more welcoming. I sat while my ears filled with Lucy's voice telling the trader that she's gone to the sea, to Cornwall, where she's now off-grid. You know we know enough, she says, to know that the City and its life-ways are not sustainable—these trees and benches are a façade of nature at best, wallpaper for our concrete plunder. Time to get out from under the shadow of the Gherkin, of all the wizards behind their glass curtains.

Modern realism asks us simultaneously to observe, but also to experience, our world in just this way; like Kostya, it asks us to mark and observe, but then also to live through, the tensions between private actions and public orientations, between what we willingly observe and what we willfully ignore. As I reached the top of Wren's Monument with the trader, the narrative gave way, for the final time, to music. The operatic quality of *AWLB* is core to its intended impact; where we normally hear horns and traffic and the sounds of the City, in our ears we now hear gentle violins, melodious arias, breaking through the noise. The contrast between these sounds helped me to recognize the

City as a potentially heterotopic space—a place where several realities might coexist at once. Atop the Monument, *AWLB* drove, for me, this message home.

On the way to the top of the Monument the trader reminded me of the fire that consumed London in 1666, and of the likelihood that, in the near future, the streets I had just walked through will be underwater, flooded as the earth's temperature rises more than two degrees Celsius. Where will humans make our homes when that happens? All of south London will be swept away, the trader said; I realized suddenly, gazing south, that my own flat would disappear. The Monument has more than 300 steps (and is not wheelchair accessible); as I climbed the tight stone walls closed in, narrower and narrower up the spiral staircase, and I reached out to steady myself. To get to the top requires the hardest physical labor of the walk; it is another, critical reminder for participants of the needs of our physical bodies, of the challenges our shared world once presented, and will again present, to our comparatively pampered modern selves.

As I emerged onto the Monument's viewing deck, the place from which we might take a "god's-eye" position of ocular command over the city at last, Stoddart's soprano broke in one last time. She sang: "We could build a new city/not on oil and gas/but on the wind and the sun"—of a place that is not a carbon-extraction enterprise, but a just and sustainable home for all. Of a place not sick but surviving, even thriving. She reminded me of the many Londons this place has already been, and still is beneath the often-oppressive concrete present: full of "possibility" just as it was when it first declared a republic in the seventeenth century, when it first "proclaim[ed] a commonwealth," and when it "inspired the world to loose the chains of slavery." Stoddart's song goes on much longer than any other music on the recording; it is with this song that *AWLB* ends. Looking out over the larger city as image, as world-picture, I was invited to imagine a different way of being in this place, and a different, fairer orientation of myself in this space than the "objective" command from on high is designed to imply.

All of the Londons of *AWLB*—the burning one of 1666, the flooded one of the near future, the carbon-blanketed one we've just walked through, the historical Londons Stoddart recalls in her song, the ancient city where Mithras once commanded his cult of Roman followers—exist together in this final moment of the walk. I found myself, quite literally, in the "heterotopia" Foucault theorizes when he articulates a space that can encompass, and place in critical dialogue, spaces seen and unseen, spaces marginal to everyday consciousness, spaces of hope. Here is also the meeting of sense and history, of multiple iterations of place and of human experiences of place, that Carlson explores as she writes of Janet Cardiff's urban audio walks as a form of shared cultural memory. This expansive ending implies that more Londons yet, ones we could build together "on hope and possibility," remain on our shared horizon. What this London might look like *AWLB* does not tell us, of course; it holds us in heterotopic space to actualize the potential, and to encourage our own future action.

Case Study #2: *Fräulein Julie*

Our second case study brings us off the streets and into the comfortable interiors of the modern theatre. In 2010, British director Katie Mitchell created a version of Strindberg's iconic naturalist drama *Miss Julie* for the Schaubühne in Berlin. This version of the play (with German text by Maja Zade) is radical in its treatment of Strindberg's stage space, revealing how that space covertly shapes the original play's narrative outcomes (which blame Julie for her masculine ambition, while celebrating Jean's social aspirations). Mitchell's treatment of the spaces of *Miss Julie* is ultimately feminist in its (re)orientation; she uses a deconstructed naturalist stage to demonstrate clearly how male and female bodies, and upper- and lower-class bodies, shape social spaces in relation one to another. *Fräulein Julie* therefore makes a spectacular example of how a naturalist conception of stage space may generate fresh political reverberations for audiences today, well over 100 years after Strindberg, Ibsen, Chekhov, and their peers sought to make the showing of the world "as it really is" revolutionary at the theatre.[1]

Fräulein Julie is an example of Mitchell's "Live Cinema" technique, an experiment in theatre-film hybridity which she began in 2006 with *Waves* (see Fowler 2017). Live Cinema features a substantial creative cast on stage; while only some of the cast act in the narrative, all members of the cast function as technical crew. There is a large projection screen at the center of the presentation space and work tables placed strategically around the stage that include Foley materials for making life-like sounds, banks of props for creating close-up images, sound booths for projecting voices, and multiple cameras. The theatre stage in Live Cinema is basically a cinematic sound-stage; the artists at work on that stage make a film of the (theatrical) text they are presenting to us, immediately before our eyes. Live Cinema thus puts both "onstage" and "backstage" worlds in front of audiences at the same time; in the process, it places those two usually clearly separated spaces into dialogue and asks spectators to understand how they actually work together to craft the representations we see on stage, and that we typically take as "natural" or given.

Fräulein Julie features an added layer of spatial complexity, relative to some other of Mitchell's Live Cinema works. At the center of its stage is a fully enclosed warren of rooms that replicate in detail (1) the kitchen space designated by Strindberg in his stage directions for the original play, (2) a bedroom for Kristin the cook (not envisioned by Strindberg, though implied in his narrative), and (3) a connecting vestibule and hallway that doubles as a performance space for a cellist who periodically contributes live music. These fully enclosed sets take very literally the "fourth wall" construction of naturalist drama; the scripted action of Strindberg's play takes place entirely inside them. Audience members can catch some glimpses of that interior action through a number of windows and doors left tantalizingly open; for the most part, however, we encounter plot developments within the set only as they are filmed for us by the team and then appear live on the screen above the stage. Not being able to see all of what is going on can be a source of frustration here; we are, after all, used to seeing in an unencumbered way at the modern theatre, being granted privileged visual access to the characters and their story. This frustration, however, is meant to be provocative and productive in Live Cinema work. We are invited to watch a great deal more than the narrative itself contains; we are thus also invited to think about how onstage and offstage spaces function in tandem to shape "realist" worlds, to think about the relationship between "given" space and "mediated" space, and to consider what kinds of labors make each kind of space possible and valuable (or not).

Mitchell has one more surprise for us. In *Fräulein Julie* it is Kristin the cook, Strindberg's minor (and least respected) character, who is the star of the show. This version refocuses the original narrative around her story, and around her interior life as she encounters the scandalous developments between Julie and Jean. Mitchell reorients the play both spatially and narratively around Kristin: she rewrites the script from her point of view, and she reorganizes the stage according to Kristin's orientation in narrative space. As Kristin inhabits the margins of the story, she inhabits the margins of the box-set: she moves in and out of the kitchen in an effort *not* to take up space, not to be unduly seen by Julie and Jean. We hover with her on its edges, waiting. Julie and Jean, meanwhile, become supporting characters; their dangerous flirtation takes place inside the box at center stage, and is offered to us only in glimpses as Kristin witnesses them through keyholes or from behind half-closed doors.

Told and shown from Kristin's perspective, *Fräulein Julie* politicizes the unseen interiors of Strindberg's drama, offering a meditation on the intersections of gender and class identity as they play out in space (and as they emerge as products *of* space). It also offers audiences a chance to reflect on how theatrical labor of all kinds organizes the spaces of naturalism to seem transparent and "given" rather than shaped by social forces. To develop my reading of the piece below, I will first unpack Live Cinema's deliberate complication of **naturalist stage space**; I will argue for its **topographical** capacity, as it invites us to learn about *how* we are privileged to see and know at the theatre, particularly about women's lives and experiences. I will then think about the relationship among actors and properties as I explore how the interactions among bodies and objects shape and reshape social space in this performance. Here, I will use a **phenomenological** approach, glancing back at Stanton Garner's arguments about realism's embodied and object-oriented qualities, to demonstrate how **Henri Lefebvre's notion of socially constructed space** works in practice, and can be observed closely in a theatre built on props and on intimate intersubjective relationships. Finally, I will consider how bodies and properties are doubled in Live Cinema in order to create Mitchell's simultaneous onstage and offstage worlds, mobilizing ideas about **theatrical ghosting** as well as prompting a potential **cultural materialist** reading of the work. As it makes space on stage for (in fact, makes its performance spaces *out of*) visibly laboring bodies, *Fräulein Julie* brings audiences into contact with the work of those whose labor we rarely see at the theatre—and which, when we do see it, we are usually asked quietly to ignore.

The Naturalist Lens: Feminist Spaces

In my discussion of genre and space in Section One, I noted that one of the most important aspects of naturalist stage topography lies in its capacity to mobilize a paradox: between intimate, embodied, and intensively object-oriented stage spaces on the one hand and a setup that privileges a forensic gaze from spectators on the other. This paradox permitted turn-of-the-twentieth-century naturalist playwrights to pose important questions about social space in a rapidly urbanizing, modernizing world, and thus to offer topographical instruction for the emerging modern subjects attending their theatres. Where is the line now between public and private? Between man and woman? Between servant and master? In a world in which God is no longer supreme, and bloodline no longer guarantees an income, how should we (*should* we?) divide our shared spaces?

Questions like these remain important for late modern audiences, but they manifest differently in a digitally driven world. Mitchell's adaptation of naturalist spatial practices accounts, first and foremost, for this difference. As twenty-first-century audiences are now accustomed to sitting in darkness at the theatre, we are no longer surprised to be granted an apparently objective position from which to gaze at a well-lit stage. We are also accustomed to enjoying screen images in relative privacy, consuming their contents without thinking about our privilege in being able to do so (or about who made the work we view, and what it might have cost or earned for them). The Live Cinema setup immediately interrupts our expectations of these now-normative processes: as we enter the auditorium, we encounter the very complex mechanisms by which images are produced for our casual consumption. The cameras, Foley tables, sound booths, and more are distributed on Mitchell's stage in order to generate the best, most life-like images of the world of the play for us to enjoy on screen. The means of image production—the things that create the very illusion of objectivity (and therefore veracity) at the cinema, at the theatre, or in front of our screens at home—are here on display, requiring a reckoning. Before the show begins, then, we see not a perfect likeness of the "real" world, but the stage-world *as a workplace for manufacturing "real" space*.

The paradox of objectivity at the naturalist theatre has long bothered feminist critics; this is because, even though avant-garde realist and naturalist practice encourages a complex spatial encounter between eye and embodiment, often the all-seeing eye of the naturalist spectator is trained directly, by naturalist narrative, on a "difficult" woman. *Miss Julie* is a case in point: Strindberg's project in this play, as he admits in his own Preface, is to diagnose Julie's problem. Jean's personal ambition (which is unquestioned as socially valuable) is used to draw out the symptoms of her physiological and hereditary pathologies while he and Julie sit, talk, and drink in the hothouse space of the intimate kitchen set. In order to refocus this doctor-patient setup (and to turn the naturalist lens away from Julie and toward Kristin), Mitchell interrupts Strindberg's framing of the fourth-wall stage as a microscope, with Miss Julie embedded in her life-like set at one end and keenly focused audience eyes at the other. She does this by doubling the stage space and exposing that space itself as a technology of seeing.

To understand exactly how this works, let's take a close look at the first few minutes of *Fräulein Julie*. The performance begins not with Strindberg's narrative but with the events leading up to the first scene; we watch Kristin undertaking her tasks in and around the kitchen in the hours before the play begins. Mitchell typically works in a rich Stanislavskian mode with her actors, asking them to imagine detailed timelines for their characters in the days, weeks, months, and even years leading up to the action of the play in order to determine their "given circumstances" in as much detail as possible and generate from their physical enactments very precise audience responses (Shevtsova 2006). Her stages are thus filled with the imagined histories of entire lives, though only glimpses of those lives will ever appear directly to spectators. In *Fräulein Julie*, the performance begins inside this actor-focused world of memory-laden things and actions: we see Kristin pluck herbs and flowers from the kitchen garden, clean the kidneys she will later feed Jean, carefully prepare the abortifacient she will give to Julie for her pregnant dog, and finally sit and wait for evening.

We are not introduced to Kristin herself right away, though. As the performance begins the lights dim to blackout, then come up first on the sound booth stage right (there is another stage left), where a woman in a modest kitchen dress sits and waits in a pool of light. Next, light rises on the Foley table stage left: two black-clad performers stand behind it. Then, light rises on another woman in a modest kitchen dress, seemingly identical to the first, standing stage right, below the sound booth, in front of a camera. At this point we hear sounds like scraping; we note that one of the Foley artists is making the sound. At last, light comes up on the screen at center stage; we see a slightly grainy image of grass, the feed from the camera downstage right. Hands enter the frame; they are the hands of the woman standing in front of the camera. The hands pluck at the grass; the sound of this action is made at the Foley table. When the owner of the hands begins to speak, it is the voice of the woman in the sound booth that we hear, overlaid onto the image on the screen.

In Section One, we explored how theatrical genre organizes the way meaning is produced through the triad of spaces that governs all theatrical experience: the space of the spectator, including our approach to the stage; the space of the stage or "set" where actors and designers work; and the interior spaces imagined by the narrative itself (the spaces of the play—the characters' world). Ghosting all three of these spaces is the normally invisible world of backstage labor—the world of fly rope operators and costume assistants acting quickly and precisely to make sure each entrance and exit happens smoothly, each scene shift is seamless. Naturalism generates its social and political power by hiding this backstage stuff in order to place stifled characters with expansive imaginations in transparently familiar, over-stuffed rooms crammed with gorgeously crafted detail; the resulting reality-effect is meant to have an uncanny and provocative impact on audience members who sit in the dark, taking it all in as before a mirror. As Mitchell observed in her director's notes in the English language program for *Fräulein Julie*, however, our topographical imaginations have adapted to this naturalist technique and are no longer penetrated by it critically. The postmodern critique of stage realism reveals that, if anything, audiences have grown skeptical of the political potential of this genre today, as its once-unique spatial configurations have become so much our norm. As if to challenge this perspective, in *Fräulein Julie*

Mitchell places all three of modernist realism's iconic spaces—the space of the stifled imagination, the space of the tight little room, *and* the space of the spectator's forensic eye—on the stage at once and lifts them, together, to our critical view. We get to see how these three imagined spaces work together to create the illusion of transparent, "given" space—the space of the real world, we might say—and we get to see what that illusion hides from us, too.

This is nowhere more evident than in the first, extended sequence of the performance featuring Kristin's kitchen labor. Note how we do not meet her as a whole, unified human subject: our first encounter with Kristin is preceded by our carefully choreographed encounter with the "backstage" labor (here placed front-and-center) that composes the image of her we see. As "she" finishes plucking her garden harvest and returns to the kitchen, the screen rises into position above stage center, revealing more of the enclosed box-set; the actor who has embodied Kristin's hands crosses to exit stage left, and lighting changes to reveal two actors working a camera setup inside the kitchen box. Eventually, the actor who "plays" Kristin (Jule Böwe) enters from stage left and moves into the kitchen's enclosed interior; we see her movements and subsequent work at sink and stove on the screen, because as an individual acting body she is not directly visible once she is inside the set. Close-ups of her work appear courtesy once more of a second Kristin, a performer placed downstage right in front of the camera seated there.

Live Cinema's fussy and constant onstage film work generates profoundly seductive screen objects; the images are romantic, intimate even, and they appear to be transparently revealing of Kristin's somewhat uneasy, yet resigned, state of mind. The screen is intended as the space where the rich interior world of Kristin's character may reside uninterrupted; it is the place where we look into Kristin's face in close-up and can imagine that we know, exactly, what she is thinking and feeling. But how can we know such things, really? After all, the actor playing Kristin is nowhere before our eyes;

she is not in our "given" space at all! The certainty of our assumption of interior knowledge at the modern realist theatre is manufactured by the orientation of realist stage space: we look from outside into life-like crammed interiors and observe in detail the interactions between characters therein. Here that conventional spatial orientation is still present, but interrupted: we must constantly decide where to look, what to look *at*. Should we pay attention to the set that blocks our view, or the screen that enables it? Should we look at the extraordinary and virtuosic creations being made in the sound-stage space between screen and audience? Our eyes are untethered; they have no focus, no ground. In this disorientation, "Kristin" the character appears plainly as a fictional figure, a technical construction of camera, light, and props—and at least two human female bodies. What we see and thus know of Kristin in this opening sequence has been carefully selected and mediated, transferred from "real" space to two-dimensional image; the mediation process, the construction of her world for artistic purposes, is what we witness, while the props and embodiments we see are those of the *makers* of personae, not the inhabitants of a complete, tragic life.

Here lies Mitchell's most significant feminist intervention into naturalist spacing practices: she shows us how the "difficult" woman shifts so easily from fictional creation to real and believable representation, according to her orientation in theatrical space. She reveals that the Miss Julies and Hedda Gablers of the naturalist canon, their psychic interiority and their cultural trauma, are products of a stage space oriented to focus our eyes consistently on them, creating the illusion of a play-world that is pre-given. Again, I want to emphasize that in its historical moment naturalism's spacing—its forced collision of audiences in intimate auditoria both with one another *and* with the narratives, bodies, and objects those audiences perhaps would rather not encounter—was socially radical and politically powerful. By feeding those historical spacing practices through the machine of Live Cinema, Mitchell updates naturalism's radical potential for a contemporary feminist theatre. She asks us to consider not *if* we know Kristin, but *how* we know her, and *why* we believe we know her so transparently. She invites us to consider what we assume about Kristin's world—and about our apparently unmitigated access, as viewers, to the women's worlds naturalism purports to offer us.

Bodies and Objects: The Construction of Social Space

Fräulein Julie deconstructs the spaces of Strindberg's play and demonstrates naturalist character—especially female character—to be a product of those spaces' orientation toward the "real" world on the one hand and spectators' eyes on the other. In another respect, however, this piece is firmly faithful to naturalist practice. Mitchell's character work with her actors is always highly detailed, grounded in material history and culture, and this work is nowhere more evident than in her extraordinarily precise use of props and objects in the shaping of characters' lives and relationships.

In Section One, we considered Henri Lefebvre's influential argument that social space is a social product, not given but constructed by embodied social relations; this can be a tricky concept to grasp in the abstract. Stanton Garner's phenomenology of theatre (also considered in Section One) goes some way help us understand how this process works: his discussion of the object-orientations of realist theatre in *Bodied Spaces* is particularly useful in this regard. Actors work with objects in order to explore and shape their own characters, and to interact with other characters in space; props mediate characters' relations and bring those relations into focus in concrete terms. Depending on the props deployed, and how they are deployed, the meanings of space in performance can shift and change, allowing our understanding of characters' relations to shift as well.

To understand more clearly how human-object relations organize social space, let's return to the first few moments of

Fräulein Julie. The labor in which Kristin is engaged when we first meet her (as hands and voice) is a very particular kind of women's work: she is making a potion to help rid Julie's dog of her pregnancy. Once the central screen has been raised and Jule Böwe enters the kitchen set, the camera inside it tracks her movements and actions. First, the camera pans slowly across the kitchen table, taking in its contents and the way the light from the window falls on the materials of Julie's work; it then lands on a chair, and on Böwe's hands. Her hands linger on the chair back, indicating Kristin may be uncertain about or uncomfortable with the work ahead—or perhaps she is just bone tired. Next, we see Böwe's hands tie an apron around her waist, from behind. The image shifts to the table again, and we see Böwe from the torso down. She ties the herbs she has brought into the house into a bundle and places them in a cheesecloth. She places the recipe book from which she is working in her apron pocket. She moves to a mirror; now we see her face, her eyes tired, about to close. This close-up is crafted downstage right, with another camera trained on the face of Kristin's double (Cathlen Gawlich). We see Böwe, inside the kitchen box, shot from behind. She places her hands on her hair, and then rubs her eyes with her fingers.

Kristin's world emerges for us as a world of objects—of kitchen objects, work objects, the things that make her kitchen a space of hard daily labor, but also a familiar place, a companion space. The object-orientation through which we discover Kristin in these early moments is not at all simple. The camera's intense focus on her body in relation to its work invites us to pay close attention to the way Kristin's hands interact with her props; through this interaction, Kristin's relationship to her employers, her lover, her history, and her future comes into focus. All of Kristin's actions in these early moments are accompanied by voice-over; the voice-over consists of lists of yet more objects—physical things she sees as well as things, memories, and ideas she imagines. "There is the apricot tree; there is the lemon tree ... there are the cicadas ... there are dreams, there are dolls," she says, often repeating items or strings of items.

"There are days, there is death" (my translations). The voice-over confirms the sense of kitchen drudgery we might perceive as we are directed to observe Böwe's hands, their work, so closely; simultaneously, however, it reveals a woman who is far more perceptive, imaginative, and socially attuned than that physical labor alone can capture.

When Kristin finishes preparing the abortifacient she carefully pours it through a funnel into a small bottle; if we pay attention we might note that she does everything she can *not* to touch the bottle with her bare skin. When she has wiped the bottle completely with a cloth she moves to the sink to rinse the cloth and then scrub her hands thoroughly. Only then does she handle the bottle, sitting in front of it, holding it, observing it almost clinically. Here, we may see Kristin momentarily as doctor, not just cook. She appears, via her engagement with the bottle, as a complex social subject, not as the "animal" Strindberg imagined, nor as only a worker, a maid. Perhaps we glimpse in her orientation toward the bottle her judgment of Julie, a woman who thinks nothing of feeding her dog poison to rid it of its unborn puppies; perhaps we glimpse her religious conviction—or her uncertainty about that conviction. Looking back on this moment from later in the performance, we may see the first hints of Kristin's own potential pregnancy. Notice how none of these glimpses are certainties, are objectively "true"; they are possibilities, deliberate reorientations of the spatial fixity of Strindberg's Kristin (whose world is either kitchen or offstage, no further). The bottle orients Kristin in relation to her paid work as a servant, but also places her in relation to Julie as a fellow woman: Julie is someone with whom she shares a fear of pregnancy; she is a woman who has the power to order her to abort a life regardless of Kristin's own qualms or convictions; and she is a woman who, in seducing Jean, may leave Kristin both economically and emotionally bereft.

After night falls, Jean enters the kitchen and the action of Strindberg's play begins. Here, props play a key role in shifting the perceived ownership of the kitchen space. It stops being Kristin's place, a familiar world that offers her a certain amount of comfort, ease, and privacy, and slowly becomes Jean and Julie's arena, a place of battle and conquest that Kristin will be forced through fatigue and discomfort to leave. Shortly after he enters the box-set, the camera reveals Jean sitting down at the table in front of his plate; Kristin moves into the shot, standing next to Jean, and dishes out the food she has prepared. She takes great care and pride, taking her time, plating the kidneys and sauce as a chef might do (to "cook" and "doctor" and "woman" we might add "artist," then). Jean protests that she has not warmed the plate; she touches his ear, but he pushes her hand away. The camera focuses on the plate, on the pan, on Jean's head in profile and on Kristin's hands wielding serving utensils, then touching Jean's body. These object and bodily interactions instantly become the bearers of spatial meaning, establishing the kitchen anew as social terrain, as class terrain, as Jean's terrain. He sits while she stands; he eats what she has cooked; he touches the plate with disdain and judges her skill. He establishes himself in these interactions as Kristin's superior, the one who holds power over this space by demanding certain actions and objects from her (a wine glass, not a beer glass). She moves; he remains still. What Kristin can do in her kitchen—what meanings her body may make or what space it may be permitted to take up—shifts radically in turn.

Once Julie enters, the kitchen's dynamic shifts again: she and Jean occupy the table as their battleground, and Kristin slumps exhausted in a chair off to one side near the wall. The camera shows her body, as so often, from the back; soon she wakes briefly, and we see her seeing Julie and Jean seated at the central table, looking half-pityingly at her. This is her cue to leave the room. From this point on, the kitchen ceases to be hers, to hold or contain or identify with her. In Strindberg's version of the story this is the point at which the actor playing Kristin exits offstage and becomes of no more consequence until morning. In Mitchell's version, however, Kristin exits the interior kitchen into a rich backstage world, into the corridors and bedroom the creative team has built for her, into the between-spaces inhabited by the creative workers of Live Cinema's workplace, into her own imagination. She exits, and she becomes of a great deal more consequence; with her, we are reoriented onto the set's creative margins.

The story told by Kristin's interactions with her props and with Jean in the first few minutes of *Fräulein Julie* is Lefebvre's story of social space as a social product. It demonstrates how space can become, and then become something else again, "through interactions, from the immensity of the global to the intimately tiny" (Massey 2005: 9). The space we call "the kitchen" only arrives on stage through interrelations: between Kristin and the bottle of poison, the chair, her notebook; between her and Jean, his plate, her pan; and between both Jean and Kristin and the looming presence of the mistress. The box-set is, in fact, just that—a set dressed for action on a stage littered with the means of theatrical representation—until it is concretized by Mitchell's actors as a living, working room in which gendered bodies and class relations collide, social identities are unmade and remade, fought for. When Kristin leaves the kitchen to enter the stage's *other* workplace, the world of cameras and Foley props and microphones, she arrives in a maker-space in which cast members literally work in furious tandem to create the seductive illusion of social space as a "given," a container for rather than shaper of identities. As they labor on the margins of the play proper, they model, by contrast, all of the spaces of the stage as necessarily interrelational, intersubjective, "contemporaneous[ly] plural," and "always under construction" (Massey 2005: 9).

The Ghosts in the Margins: Theatre's Hidden Laborers

All theatre props bear narrative meaning and orient stage space as they organize social relations, as we have just seen, but they also do more. Props are fundamental markers of theatrical labor: actors work with them in rehearsal as well as in performance, using them to build the character we will eventually observe. It is also work to get props onto the stage in the first place—that labor is performed by props and costume workers on the technical crew. Technical labor at the theatre ghosts artistic labor because it is essential, but it is not meant to be seen: this is why stage hands wear black, to blend into the set they create, and why the names of crew persons run far down the list of credits in theatre programs, if they appear at all. (Ironically, Mitchell costumes *Fräulein Julie*'s non-narrative cast—those who perform technical work on stage, but do not appear in the play's story—in black, in a nod to the modern theatre convention of rendering technical, logistical labor invisible. Of course, her technical "cast" is among the most virtuosic performers in *Fräulein Julie*, the true stars of the show, from whom it is a struggle to pull our eyes.)

At the end of Section One I discussed performance theory's investment in discourses of ghosting, the way performance spaces can bear the traces of bodies, props, and stories that have come before. I linked that discussion to site-specific theatre practice in particular; it is a late modern genre invested in animating performatively the ghosts of a given location. Sites are often chosen for the potential latent in a space's past; work made for the site may directly or indirectly invoke past events or occupants in order to make a political claim about the space's value, meaning, or cultural purpose.

In transforming a naturalist drama into a film set, Mitchell turns *Fräulein Julie*'s stage into a "site": one that invites audiences to think critically about the ways in which space shapes character, as we have just seen, but also one that thinks critically about the many kinds of labor that usually travel, unmarked and unacknowledged, through theatre spaces of all kinds. In this respect, the "ghosting" and "site-specific" elements of this performance encourage a cultural materialist reading of Mitchell's Live Cinema. (Note, however, that a full cultural materialist reading of the piece would also ask important extra-theatrical questions, such as: Are all the performers on stage paid the same rate? How are they acknowledged in the program? Does the labor of making the show [i.e., rehearsal labor] impact all performers in the show similarly? Are there behind-the-scenes workers we do not see, and who are not acknowledged to the same degree as those performing onstage cinematic work? It would then weave the answers to these questions into its assessment of how the show's performed labor is represented on stage to audiences.)

Both bodies and props are doubled in Live Cinema; every item operating within the narrative is connected directly to a series of "offstage" persons and objects. These bodies and items point beyond themselves: to their cinematic doubles in the offstage spaces of the prop and Foley tables, to the duplicate items used to make close-up images possible, and to the sonically analogous items used to produce the sounds of everyday action and use. Every prop or body in the performance thus operates in multiple spaces simultaneously, drawing our attention keenly to the way the narrative, onstage, and offstage worlds of a play are intimately, irrevocably linked by shared, human labor.

When Kristin the character exits the narrative as Böwe the actor exits the box-set kitchen, they join, both ontologically and materially, the creative team building the images we see on the margins of the set. Ejected from Strindberg's narrative, Kristin/Böwe becomes part of the performance's *other* working spaces, the spaces where the challenging, complicated, hidden work of making naturalism's transparent "reality" takes place. Kristin, we need to remember, is the play's preeminent invisible laborer: she is a kitchen maid; she is abused by Jean, her social equal; her place in the world of the play is given no thought by either Jean or Julie as they ignore her to pursue their own desires. Further, as a character Kristin is required by Strindberg to do a certain amount of unpaid heavy lifting inside the narrative: though he disdains her (in his Preface) as base and stupid in her devotion to social codes and religious propriety, he needs her in order to make Jean and Julie's dalliance come crashing down to earth in the play's final scene, as they reenter the material world whose boundaries are determined by those very codes.

In her many kinds of work, physical and ethical, on stage and off, Kristin is *Fräulein Julie*'s ghost: she shares this in common with other invisible theatrical laborers who travel unseen between the spaces of narrative and the spaces of narrative's construction. In Mitchell's Live Cinema version of her story, Kristin's spectral place is clearly marked as such, just as the labor of those supporting the on-screen narrative is clearly marked and celebrated as virtuosic, not superfluous (nor to be hidden). This is a feminist gesture, as well as a site-specific one. Mitchell reorients the spaces of Strindberg's play not only around Kristin, but around the invisible work her character is based upon. That includes Kristin's literal work, as well as the work—physical labor, emotional labor, manual labor—it takes to represent her as either fixed or mobile, as either trapped in the Count's kitchen in a strict naturalist rendering of the play, or as moving between the spaces of labor and the spaces of its representation in the Live Cinema version of her story.

Case Study #3: *The Shipment*

Our final extended case study in this section focuses on *The Shipment*, created in 2008–9 by Young Jean Lee, a Korean American writer and director, in conjunction with an all-Black team. Lee's collaborators in the creation of the show included the original cast—Mikeah Ernest Jennings, Prentice Onayemi, Okieriete Onodowan, Douglas Scott Streater, and Amelia Workman—as well as Jordan Barbour, Joi Anissa Favor, JoiLynn, Antyon Le Monte Smith, and Stephen McIntosh.[2] The show is divided into two parts, which the company describes like this:

> The first half is structured like a minstrel show—dance, stand-up routine, sketches, and a song—and was written to address the stereotypes the cast members felt they had

> to deal with as black performers. For the second half of the show, Lee asked the actors to come up with roles they'd always wanted to play, and wrote a naturalistic comedy in response to their requests. (Lee 2009)

At first glance, *The Shipment* might seem an odd choice for a spatial analysis. Unlike *And While London Burns* (*AWLB*), it does not require audiences to leave a "traditional" theatre space and engage physically and affectively with the urban locales in and about which the performance is made. Unlike *Fräulein Julie*, it does not immediately and apparently transform the stage into a labor-intensive "site," juxtaposing theatre as a workplace with theatre as a space of representation in order to invite audience members to think about what that juxtaposition can tell us. In fact, audience members with no prior knowledge of *The Shipment* or the political impulses behind its development could be forgiven, as they take their seats, for imagining that it is simply a comedy show, simply designed for their enjoyment.

Look again at the brief description offered in the quotation above. Notice, as you re-read it, that it contains a clue about the spatial interventions *The Shipment* offers. The description focuses on two things: the actors' lived experience of their race on the one hand, and the role played in this lived experience by theatrical genre on the other. The first half of the piece "is structured like a minstrel show"; in it, Black actors will play roles into which they have historically been written by the social, political, and economic forces of institutionalized racism. They will take up the places history has offered Black actors at the theatre: stereotypes of buffoonery, crass and foul-mouthed, riddled with apparent criminal intent. In the second half, however, the work will switch gears to present a "naturalistic comedy." The roles provided for by this genre are exactly the kinds of roles Lee's actors expressed a wish to play, but which they hadn't been given the chance to play before. Because theatre history doesn't typically associate "naturalistic comedy" with Blackness, Black bodies are—culturally and historically—perceived to be "out of place" in such works. (The actor didn't "fit" the role, we might imagine a well-intentioned director of Ibsen or Chekhov remarking.) As we will see below, *The Shipment*'s second half gains its political force precisely from the disjunction between the Black bodies performing its characters, and the fact that, historically, those bodies would not have been permitted, expected—nor even imagined!—to *take up a place* in a naturalistic comedy.

AWLB allowed us to explore the ways in which our experiences of urban space are always impacted, and perhaps even structured, by the forces of capitalism: by those forces' power to designate so much of our shared world as "private property" and to ravage that property at will. *Fräulein Julie* allowed us to think about how space is organized by labor, and how the social operations of class and gender in space shape who "belongs" to what spaces, and who haunts the margins. *The Shipment* will now allow us to recognize how the forces of racism shape social, economic, and political spaces—and in particular how the forces of racism shape the ordering of theatrical space, both the worlds imagined by a script on stage and the differently designated spaces (onstage, offstage, auditorium space) inside a theatre building.

Below I will read three episodes from *The Shipment*: the initial, stand-up comedy sequence that is performed in the online archive video by Douglas Scott Streater; the "naturalistic comedy" sequence of the second half; and the performance of the Modest Mouse song "Dark Center of the Universe" that marks the bridge between the two parts of the show. Although I will note throughout the ways in which genre organizes and lends meaning to the spaces the performers inhabit, I will not focus predominantly on genre as a spatial technology here. Instead, I will first turn to **the legacy of Aristotle** to help us think about how theatrical performance charges the spaces between audience and performer, the spaces of catharsis—which, as I noted in Section One, are always political spaces, whether a performance marks them as political or not. Then, I'll look at the second half of *The Shipment* through

Turner's "topographic" lens; I'll talk about how this part of the performance uses existing, often unacknowledged audience expectations about which kinds of bodies "belong" to the spaces of naturalism in order to teach us about how spatial configurations at the theatre shape our understanding of race and space beyond the theatre. Finally, looking at the song bridge, I'll take up **Doreen Massey's notion of space as culturally relational**, as structured by bodies whose different allocations in and habitations of social space organize the ways in which we perceive those bodies as holding value, as threatening shared values, or as without value at all.

Geopathology—theatre's *failure* to provide a home for all bodies, for all imagined worlds, despite its frequent promise to do so—also haunts *The Shipment*, predominantly through the violence and trauma invoked by the piece's somewhat cryptic name. What is a shipment, after all, but cargo, objects in space, moving between one place and another? Here, the word "shipment" conjures the bodies of Black men, women, and children stolen from their homes and shipped across the ocean to the Americas during the trans-Atlantic slave trade. It also, however, invokes the image of a parcel—maybe anticipated, but maybe more than we bargained for—landing on an unsuspecting doorstep, cargo with an undeniable presence with which we must now engage, for which we must now *make space* in our own homes and imaginings. Finally, then, I'll argue that what *The Shipment* leaves us with is a sense not of theatre's racial pathologies but of its truest and deepest heterotopic potential: a sense of what the theatre might look like if its spaces were inhabited, comfortably and easily, by different kinds of bodies, bringing differently embodied histories to bear on those spaces' mimetic potential every day.

This argument will provide a route for us into the concluding section of the book, in which I will suggest that the next step in theatre studies' "spatial turn" must be to reckon with what it would mean truly to decolonize theatrical space in postcolonial and settler colonial places like the United States, Canada, Great Britain, Australia, and beyond.

From Catharsis to Discomfort: The Aristotelian Lens

You might at first imagine Aristotle's theory of tragedy—with its focus on unity of action, and its emphasis on audience catharsis (releasing strong emotions like pity or fear)—to be an unlikely choice as a theoretical framework for thinking about a Black male performer's stand-up comedy routine. And yet, in his fifteen-minute monologue at the beginning of *The Shipment*, Douglas Scott Streater plays cunningly both with the "improbable" (what "can" or "should" happen at a comedy show) and with the power and potential of catharsis (what audience members "can" or "should" be encouraged to feel at a comedy show) as he draws spectators into his schtick—only to forcefully and jarringly push them away again. If you revisit now the "Backstory" I discuss at the top of Section One, you'll recall that Aristotle's interest in unity of action and his focus on catharsis as tragedy's ideal outcome are space-saving impulses: Aristotle suggests that maintaining a unified, closed structure of action and emotion at the theatre allows—in theory—for audience members to experience the world as it "ought" to be, and not to allow their imaginations to stray too far beyond the "probable." Probability, as I note, is primarily a conservative injunction about who gets to take up what kinds of space: let us not have bodies on stage where they do not belong; let us not imagine women or slaves in positions they "could" not inhabit in "real" life, lest things get confusing.

Streater appears at roughly the three-minute mark; he bounces onto the stage lip, the majority of the space behind him entirely black (as it will be for all of the first half of the show). Loud, aggressive rap music accompanies him; he smiles but makes rude gestures (at one point he pulls down his pants and wiggles his bum at the audience), along with some winsome dance moves. He's having fun being a bit of a douche. He plays the familiar figure of the Black stand-up comic who will perform certain stereotypes (the foul-mouthed "motherfucker"; the "gangsta"; the goofing clown) inherited from the nineteenth-century minstrel tradition (which featured versions of all of these kinds of roles—Blacks as harmless and idiotic, Blacks as an existential threat).[3]

Contemporary stand-up comedy shares a central spatial dynamic with minstrel and variety shows from the nineteenth and early twentieth centuries. Both trade on the simultaneous division of the theatre space into performer's space and audience space, and the constant transgressing of that division: the stand-up comic works at and usually paces up and down along the lip of the stage, referencing people in the audience frequently, just as variety performers use the stage to showcase their virtuosity but nevertheless seek our laughter, applause, and approval directly. In this sense, the division between spectacle and spectator in this kind of shared variety format is not really a division at all: the goal of the performer, especially in stand-up, is to become comfortably familiar with the audience, to bring us, by way of some uncomfortable moments along the way, to the ultimate comfort of relieving laughter. Comedy and variety shows actually work best when they collapse the distance between performer and observer in the service of shared, ultimately pleasurable emotion, just as Aristotle's unities operate to encourage audience members to experience a shared, ultimately pleasurable catharsis. Both work in the service of preserving certain status quos.

Streater's act presents us with this familiar setup, and therefore with the familiar expectation that the difference between (Black) performer and (at best mixed, but probably majority White) audience will ultimately appear as no real difference at all—the material fact of racial difference will collapse into our laughing enjoyment as his act proceeds for our pleasure. However, almost instantly Streater begins to manipulate our expectations. His first extended joke is about lesbian sex between underage girls, and the pleasure he took (as a teenager) in watching it; immediately, he breaks a social taboo. The early, raucous audience laughter dies down considerably. Streater "rescues" this fail (an obviously intentional one) by calling attention to the fact that the audience may now regard him as a "pedophile"; he makes a joke and moves back into familiar, more comforting territory. Next, he makes another typical, expected joke about White vs. Black people having sex; once more he swiftly turns the tables on the audience, though, when the White couple in his story are revealed to be having sex not with each other but with goats. Again, the audience's laughter see-saws.

Streater proceeds like this—disrupting our enjoyment just enough to make something about his routine seem not quite right, or is it just us?—until the ten-minute mark. That's when he says, "White people always gotta be beastin!" He calls "beastin" "semi-ironic hip-hop lingo" (to warm laughter) and defines it like this: "Beastin is when I call you out on your racist bullshit, and you turn around and say that I'm the one that's got the problem" (10:02–10:26). This marks the halfway point in Streater's routine, which until now has gently raised the specter of White racism and Black cultural stereotypes, but always with the kind of familiarity that allows audience members to be "in" on the moment, near to and in league with the comic rather than against him. Now, Streater's tone shifts the dynamics of the space entirely: his face becomes fixed and angry, his tone raging. He *yells* at the audience:

> THAT'S BEASTIN. JUST BEIN' A BEAST!
> So I'm gonna say what I gotta say and, fuck it. If you don't like it [points stage left] LEAVE!
> This is my show. If you don't like it, LEAVE!

These lines are punctuated by heavy pauses; the longest pause follows the last line. Nobody in the audience laughs, or makes any audible noise; the silence reveals no clues as to what kinds of emotions audience members may be feeling, or what they might be thinking. It does, however, imply that the space between comic and audience has become strangely charged, rendered unfamiliar, made uncomfortable to a degree that leaves behind the boundaries of "comfortable discomfort" usually associated with stand-up. Unlike in a typical routine, here Streater seeks not to transmit "funny" directly from his words and actions to our ears, yielding a consensus of laughter. Instead, his words and gestures claim the space of the stage for himself, putting the audience, figuratively and literally, in its place. With Streater in "his" place ("this is my show") and the audience in its own, very different one ("if you don't like it, leave!"), the act then goes on to explore how space is owned and claimed, by some bodies more than others, both at the theatre and in the world beyond it.

Streater's "beastin" sequence exposes the contradictory power dynamics underlying his familiar setup, and indeed underlying any theatrical setup that claims a particular kind of unity: in material fact, the comic is *always* in charge of the performance space, both his and his spectators', even though stand-up trades on the apparent collapse of this space into homogeneous familiarity, and on the notion that the audience can determine with their laughter (or lack of it) when the comic's time is up. Here, Streater's difference—as a Black man who must perform particular stereotypes in order to generate laughter in White or dominant-culture identified audiences—emerges to *takes up space* in an overt, disquieting way that renders it not funny, but (literally) powerful. Regardless of how you react, Streater insists, this space is mine for this period of time, and I hold the power to stay. If you do not like my occupation, you can leave. As the genre of his speech shifts, the room itself shifts: it becomes a different kind of performance space, one in which spectators are not even nominally in charge.

Like Kristin, as she leaves the kitchen set to Jean and Julie in Mitchell's production, and like Lucy and the Trader in *AWLB*, who toil in the bowels of late capital even as it destroys the home they cherish, Streater performs in a space designated *for* his labor, but to which as a Black actor he has very limited occupancy rights. To dwell there, in normal times, he must solicit our comfort and laughter; if we do not laugh he must leave. By turning the tables on us he reveals that our laughter, in normal times, supports a status quo in which Black bodies are too often made to perform for White expectations; it supports a conservative, and in fact oppressive, worldview in which Black bodies must conform to White imaginings about how social and political space is ordered, and about what places Black bodies "ought to" take up within that space. Normal times are about what Aristotle would call probability; they afford little room for imagining alternative spatial possibilities.

Race and the Topographic Stage

The first half of this 85-minute show ends at the 38-minute mark. Streater's act is followed by a video-game-style gangsta sequence about a young Black boy falling into drug dealing and violence; that sequence gives way to the song bridge I'll discuss in the final part of this case study. The space and tone of the performance then shift significantly once more: a living room set straight out of a conventional realist comedy arrives on stage, complete with a leather sofa, bar cart, decorative plants, books arranged for display, and seating for at least five characters. (The set transition, which is performed by un-costumed stagehands and accompanied by Mary J. Blige's "Ooh" [2003], happens in full audience view, as part of the show; there is no interval.)

When the lights come back up on the set, two smartly dressed Black men (Streater as Thomas and Mikeah Ernest Jennings as Omar) are seated on the sofa. They are talking about Omar's diet: he eats no dairy and no meat, but eggs and fish. Thomas asks if he eats butter; Omar notes, with perverse glee, that he uses olive oil instead, even on his toast. Michael seems baffled by all of this, while Omar displays extraordinary, very loud enthusiasm for the topic under discussion. He wears a bright waistcoat under his suit, white top-siders, and he sports a slightly chaotic-looking Afro that makes him seem, along with his high-pitched, loud voice, just a little bit like a clown. The audience laughs frequently and raucously at both his enthusiasm and Thomas's bewilderment.

As in Streater's monologue, everything on stage at this early moment appears, on the surface, to conform to type: the set and the conversation, as well as the laughter cues, all fit familiar patterns. They could be from a Noël Coward play, or from a TV show like *Friends*: they are situation comedy. The setting (the world created by the stage hands during the transition sequence) as well as the interior world of the story (that which Streater and Jennings set up with their chat on the couch) both jive: they orient us in space, toward a particular kind of performance ("naturalistic comedy," as the Young Jean Lee website description puts it), and ultimately toward a particular kind of outcome—after some conflict, happy resolution. They encourage us to settle in and watch without worry. And yet, something is not quite right: Omar's extreme excitement about his diet, his loud voice, and the Afro matched with his dandyish waistcoat and top-siders don't quite "go" together. Streater's reaction confirms this. They are—he is—disorienting.

Recall my discussion in Section One about how we enter Shakespeare's Globe theatre. There, I talked about how the ways audiences are invited into a theatre building cue our orientation in theatrical space, our expectations of what will come, even before a performance begins. At the Globe, I noted, audiences emerge from narrow darkness into vast, communal light; this orientation matches the Globe's mandate to open worlds up at the theatre, to show audience members of all backgrounds the many worlds they *may* inhabit. At modern proscenium arch theatres, by contrast, audience members sit in the darkness and their eyes are oriented toward the lights on stage, and thus toward the ocular vanishing point at the dead center of that stage. While modernist realism is not quite as uniformly directed as this built orientation may ideally imply, as a genre it encourages an individualized, forensic, and privileged viewpoint, one in which audience members experience a proximity to the represented world on stage that may be either familiar or uncomfortable—or, in the best naturalist work, often both at once. These kinds of physical orientations help to generate Henry Turner's "topographic" stage, transforming the theatre building and its internal spaces into a place of learning about the organization of the world through the process of inhabiting and experiencing different, even conflicting, representations of that world on the stage.

In the second half of *The Shipment*, Lee and her cast play deliberately with the line between "familiar" and "uncomfortable" inherent to naturalism in order to generate for audiences an uncanny experience that leads to very specific learning about what makes "naturalistic comedy" work as a genre. This is a learning about what kinds of bodies have, historically, been permitted to inhabit a realistic-looking set as main characters, and what bodies are relegated (often still today) to the margins—literally—of mainstream theatre in minor roles like maids or butlers. The performance's mission, in other words, is explicitly topographical: it shows us a conventional, realist representation of our world at the mainstream theatre in order to explore how our normative relationships to race organize those very representations, as well as the extra-theatrical worlds they reference.

As new characters enter the living room set, each of them seems slightly off-putting, like Omar. Prentice Onayemi's Desmond, for example, is dressed in a tuxedo, yet behaves like a robot, speaking in brisk monotones about entirely banal topics. Amelia Workman as Thomasina plays the "straight" woman in a swish party dress, reacting with surprise, disdain, or discomfort to the shenanigans of the others on stage. Though she is welcome in this mix as a seemingly normal guest, she becomes increasingly mean and unlikeable in her speech and actions. (She throws me off guard with this behavior, and I find I do not identify with her, despite our shared gender and class status—this is an important, deliberate disruption of realism's iconicity on the part of the show.) Meanwhile, the farcical elements of the plot escalate the weirdness. Thomas reveals to his assembled guests that it is his thirtieth birthday; he exits abruptly and returns with a cake; the group sings happy birthday, awkwardly; Thomas then licks the candles aggressively before smashing bits of the cake into his face.

Omar accuses Thomasina of accusing Thomas of being drunk; an uncomfortable, wide-ranging argument about the characters' personal lives, habits, and problems ensue. Thomas then announces that he has poisoned his guests' drinks. After several minutes of panic and anger, with Omar phoning for an ambulance, Thomas reveals that he is "just fucking" with them—because he is miserable and because he believes if they leave he will kill himself.

This is, on one level, standard living room farce; at the point of Thomas's breakdown, however, things shift toward the serious, the very human, the intimately familiar. Sitting at the lip of the stage with a bottle of liquor, Thomas talks about being lonely, hating his job, feeling old, and wanting more. "Sometimes I need physical contact so badly I think I'll die," he says (1:13:19); this is something most of us in the audience can easily relate to. The other guests are only somewhat sympathetic, making the audience perhaps even more so, as Thomas seems alienated. Eventually, the other guests agree to play a game to lighten the mood. Thomas suggests "Library," in which one player chooses a book, shows the cover, explains what the book is, and then the other guests make up lines they would expect to be in that book. After a warm-up round, Thomas discovers a book called *Black Magic*, which contains a chapter called "Negro Superstitions." The chapter contains lists of superstitions, and each participant must make one up, starting their fantasy superstition with the phrase: "The Negro believes …"

Everyone thinks hard; Thomasina glances into the distance and begins to laugh. "I'm going to hell," she says as she scribbles her response; "I'm so going to hell for this" (1:22:29–34). Thomas gathers everyone's papers; the first piece he reads out says, "The Negro believes cod liver oil cures cancer." The second contains only the words "The Negro believes"—someone has come up with nothing, or perhaps just does not want to play (likely, this is Omar). Other superstitions are similarly forced (the answers are not really funny). Thomas then reads Thomasina's superstition out loud. It is: "the Negro believes that the Negro's hands and feet are white because 'da moon da'nt touch dem in Africa'" (1:23:35–45). Thomas laughs hysterically; Thomasina looks around, smug. Desmond joins in late, his laughter too loud, robotic again, ridiculous. Then, Omar says:

> I'm sorry, I'm sorry, I have to say that I'm really uncomfortable with all of this. I just don't think we'd be doing this if there was a Black person in the room. (1:24:00)

Desmond responds: "I guess that would depend on what kind of Black person it was." The moment (and the play) ends in a swift blackout.

If we now read the entire comedy backward through this surprise "reveal," the blend of familiar and strange peppered throughout its highly conventional setup becomes visible as a deliberate disorientation tactic. Omar and Desmond have been hilarious in their oddity all along not only because their vocal and gestural behavior does not "fit" with the naturalist norm—it's because their Black bodies do not "fit" our normative perception of the middle-class, young and affluent framework that makes this piece a naturalistic comedy in the first place. (A clown and a robot, arguably, are as weird in this setup as two twenty-something Black men—therein lies the painful rub.) The strangeness of Thomas having a (presumably quite old) racist book about "Negroes"—and wanting to make a silly game of it, that everyone is willing to play along with—suddenly clicks. The moments of uncanniness we've been experiencing, as we laugh on cue to stuff that's not that funny, or feel connected to Thomas's very human misery, rush to the foreground: the actors' *bodies* are Black, but the *characters* they are playing are White. In their Whiteness they are familiar. In their Blackness they are *literally out of place*. The characters are White because Black characters are not perceived, easily or typically, to belong to the worlds represented on stage—to "mainstream" or "middle class" or "realist" worlds, except as butlers or maids, sidekicks, or friends. The bodies are Black because the subtext of the piece is not about pleasure, but learning: learning about how race organizes space as "normal" or "strange," learning about how the configuration of social space identifies raced bodies as either belonging, or not belonging, and then puts them (keeps them) in their place.

Think now of Trayvon Martin, shot in Sanford, Florida in February 2012 by George Zimmerman, a neighborhood watch volunteer. Martin was shot because his body and the color of his skin were read by Zimmerman as not belonging to the suburban, gated community where he was walking, while visiting relatives who lived in that community. Martin's Black body was read by Zimmerman as not just out of place, but as dark and dangerous, a threat to the community. He read Martin's body as "threat to space," not "of this place"; he fired his gun.

If middle-class worlds, family communities, are understood by default in Euro-American culture as White, then not only are they likely to be scripted for the stage or screen with White characters, but they are likely to be cast with White actors, too. Black actors in such roles would lend—as they do in *The Shipment*, in a deliberately tangible way—a strangeness, an assumed *improbability*, to the picture of transparent Whiteness we have been schooled by so much realist theatre about couples, families, and their conflicts to expect. Black bodies would seem other-worldly—other than the world-as-given, place-as-usual. They would be less "relatable" to audiences assumed to be White, affluent, or middle-class—or so the argument in casting sessions often goes. (This is the same argument that says films or TV shows or plays by or about women are less bankable because they are only "relatable" to women.)

The second half of *The Shipment* organizes its stage space in order to play with the White-world-as-usual trope that has so long governed mainstream theatrical space in the North and West of the planet. It challenges the idea that Black bodies cannot, should not, be perceived as "like" or "near to" the audiences that inhabit those spaces—that they are too "other" to communicate information about worlds that are not explicitly framed as Black worlds, inherently out of place in the spaces that White creators and audiences have so long dominated and imagined as their own. The farce that ends *The Shipment* reclaims the spaces of naturalism for Black bodies, much as Mitchell's *Fräulein Julie* reclaims Strindberg's naturalist "masterpiece" for female domestic labor, for invisible labor of all kinds at the theatre. Simultaneously, it reveals the notion of characters' perceived relatability to be based on a series of assumptions about *bodies in space*: that some bodies belong, while other bodies are too far away, too other to reflect me, to connect to me—on the notion, in other words, that Black bodies have no place in our world at all.

What Does This Place Stand For?[4]

In the sequence that bridges the minstrel show in the first half of *The Shipment* and the naturalistic comedy in the second, three actors (including Prentice Onayemi and Amelia Workman) move to the front and center of the stage, stand still, and stare. They do not stare at the audience; they stare into the space *between* the audience and the stage. This is the space that Streater charged with political force and conviction in his comic monologue. It is also the space that is supposed to disappear when the comedy begins, sinking us into its comfortable world. They stand, dressed in black suits and a night-sky-blue silk dress, against the black background, empty but for their bodies. They stare into the black that separates us, Black bodies and not-Black bodies, racially marked and unmarked bodies. They see the gulf and address it.

The actors stand and stare for over a minute (33:32–34:45). Then, Workman breaks the silence. She sings the opening words from Modest Mouse's 2000 song, "Dark Center of the Universe." Workman sets the tone: her voice is slow, without affect, yet melodious. She sounds worn, tired—almost as if she has had to sing this song many times before. The men join her, and an acapella, three-part harmony ensues; the men keep their hands in their pockets while Workman's hands hang straight at her side. The performers make no gestures or other movement to accompany their song; like Streater's monologue, it is both a pleasure, delightful to hear (as Aristotle might say), and yet troubled, troubling, a challenge to engage. The motionless bodies and blank stares clash with the lovely harmonies. The bodies, their gorgeous voices, seem to fit, and yet clearly they do not fit. They refuse, actively, to perform as they sing—they refuse to fit in, to fit themselves to expectation.

In Section One, I considered Doreen Massey's important contribution to post-Lefebvrian human geography, and in particular her influential argument that space is "the product of interrelations; as constituted through interactions" (2005: 9). I noted that, for Massey, these interactions crucially include those that take place across class, gender, race, and ethnicity. Elsewhere in her introduction to *For Space*, Massey elaborates:

> Space does not exist prior to identities/entities and their relations. More generally I would argue that identities/entities, the relations "between" them, and the spatiality which is part of them, are all co-constitutive. ... *the very possibility of any serious recognition of multiplicity and heterogeneity itself depends on a recognition of spatiality.* (10–11, my emphasis)

As they sing Modest Mouse's indie-rock hit in this raw, stripped-down way, Workman and the other performers offer exactly such a "recognition of spatiality" in an attempt to spark a "serious recognition of multiplicity" among their listeners. The song is obviously work for them—their banal, unenthusiastic affect ensures we understand this—and a large part of that work has to do with the labor the lyrics demand. Notice that this labor is about space; the lyrics are, literally, *about space*. (If you don't know the song, please stop reading and go listen to it now. Copyright restrictions prevent me from quoting the lyrics here.)

With the song's first lines the singers tell us they would disintegrate, disappear into thin air, leave this place without a trace if "we" want them to; they are not the "dark center" of the universe we may have imagined them to be, the black hole that might one day swallow all human place, disintegrating the world as we know it. Remember Trayvon Martin once more; think about how easily, how routinely, so many North Americans (and Britons, and Europeans) render Black bodies invisible, for example when considering who is, or who should be, in the room when important social and political decisions are made. On the other side of the same racial coin, consider how easily those same individuals imagine, like George Zimmerman did that night in Sanford, an ordinary, human Black body to be the outsized container of the greatest human fears, an existential threat to both security of place and security of being.

Workman and her peers sing that they are neither of these things—neither no place, nor all space. (They are not, will never be forced into, the sunken place.[5]) Their simultaneously hopeful and exhausted, frank yet bland voices, coupled with their very basic human stances (feet on ground, hands at side or in pocket, torsos facing front, shoulders back), remind us they are indissoluble in their difference to a White audience, but also insistent in their co-presence here with that audience. They are bodies in space, bodies that take up the space a human body occupies—no less or more. Massey writes: "Precisely because space ... is a product of relations-between ... it is always in the process of being made. It is never finished; never closed. Perhaps we could imagine space as a simultaneity of stories-so-far" (2005: 9). What stories could Black bodies show and tell if given the chance to be seen and heard in their proper difference, their entirely human occupation of space upon the earth? If they did not need to fear invisibility and disintegration, banishment from the spaces White bodies make so comfortable for one another?

The song ends; the actors hold their stares for a moment, then walk away. They are neither themselves nor their (several) characters in this leaving moment; instead, they hold open the space between performer and character, between the demand to perform and its refusal, as they hold open the space race makes between the lip of the stage and the first row of seats. In that hold is a call to a politics: a call to think directly, clearly, about how racially marked bodies frame the physical and imagined spaces of our world, at but also far beyond the theatre. In that hold is another demand, too: that we in the audience watch the "naturalistic comedy" to come with different eyes, with eyes that can see difference, properly. That we try to hear and see, in a very familiar setup, not only the stories-so-far, but the stories that yet may come.

SECTION THREE

Towards a Decolonized Stage

In this concluding section of the book, I will look ahead to one possible direction for the future of the "spatial turn" in theatre and performance studies: I will ask what it might mean to decolonize the spaces of the Anglo-European ("Western") stage.

Here, I will explicitly take up the promise and the challenge I invoked at the end of my discussion of *The Shipment*. As we saw at the end of Section Two, *The Shipment* snakes into the comfortable spaces of traditional variety shows and naturalist comedies only to satirize them darkly; its ironic use of space reveals the ways in which these generic theatre structures uphold normalized configurations of Blackness and Whiteness, and thus the violence and injustice those configurations perpetrate both inside and outside the theatre. *The Shipment*'s stark politicization of Anglo-European stage space (including the space between actor and audience, typically a space of safe distance, which the show charges with fear, uncertainty, disquiet, and potential violence) demands that spectators try to see the work on stage from perspectives other than the usual, to sit with their emerging discomfort and try to understand it. It demands that we try to see and feel and perhaps even inhabit quotidian space differently, more justly, by working to understand how space orients our bodies, and how it orients some bodies toward safety while it directs others toward danger. But: what would it mean to do—*really do*—this work of spatial renovation in the name of social and racial justice? How might Kevin Hetherington's theoretical heterotopia—the promise of a space of "alternate ordering"—become lived reality? For whom, and by whom, should this work be undertaken, and for whose benefit?

For the members of more than 5,000 Indigenous nations located in more than seventy-five countries around the globe (Snelgrove, Dhamoon, and Corntassel 2014: 13), this question is not rhetorical, nor abstract, nor immaterial. It is a matter of fair and just representation; it is a matter of human rights. Indigenous populations worldwide have had not only their worldviews, but also the literal ground of their worlds—their lands; their claims to those lands as homes, as workplaces, and as sources of spiritual and physical sustenance; their sovereign rights to steward those lands—stolen from them by the practices of settler colonialism. Those populations continue to be dispossessed by the ongoing refusal of so-called "postcolonial" nations (such as Canada, Australia, and the United States) to return First Nations lands to Indigenous sovereignty, or to grant the First Peoples of those lands the right to protect them from, among other things, ecologically devastating resource extraction.

Along with this theft of land has come much more: a theft of family ties, lineages, and community lifeways. This theft has taken place, for example, through the forced relocation of Indigenous children to residential schools, where their languages and rituals were forbidden; it has taken place through an outlawing of traditional cultural and performances practices, such as the coastal longhouse potlatch, deemed too foreign or "uncivilized" for the likings of colonial overlords.[1] The theft of land, for Indigenous peoples around the world subject to settler-colonial dispossession, has thus gone hand-in-hand with the theft of the means of representation; settler colonialism is frequently accompanied by cultural genocide. For First Peoples living under settler colonialism, "space" is not just an idea, then, sometimes abstract and sometimes more precise and local; it is a resource for survival, a means of community-building, a means of self-governance, a communal history, a relationship to ancestry, as well as a means of individual subject-formation.

In the context of redress for both territorial and cultural violence against Indigenous peoples, decolonizing the stage therefore requires fundamentally reorienting the theatrical spaces on which Indigenous experiences are presented, for Indigenous as well as settler audiences. It requires re-conceiving space *from an Indigenous point of view*: using Indigenous epistemologies and cosmologies to (re)create at the theatre the spaces in which Indigenous lifeways may be practiced, rehearsed, and remembered, in a project of cultural "survivance" (Vizenor 1999; Carter 2015) rather than settler edification. Decolonizing the stage may therefore be understood as one among many vital practices directed materially toward reclaiming the lands, and the worldviews, ripped from First Peoples by the practices of settler colonization.

Theatrical decolonization is an ongoing project, not one with a definitive trajectory or a simple solution. In any case, it should not, and cannot, fall to me as a White settler writer and theorist to speak to its most fundamental questions about process or ownership. What I will offer in the pages ahead, then, is an example of one way we might approach potential decolonization at the contemporary Canadian theatre, using a theoretical model drawn primarily from the Indigenous (Stó:lō) musicologist Dylan Robinson. Using Robinson's work (and related work by Indigenous and allied scholars in theatre studies) alongside my experience as an academic and settler spectator, I will offer a close reading of *Kiinalik: These Sharp Tools* (2017), a recent performance staged at Buddies in Bad Times Theatre in Toronto. *Kiinalik* drew on an array of strategies for respectfully de-centering settler audience members, along with their assumptions and expectations about their "place" at a theatre event that presented Indigenous experiences. At the same time, it reoriented spectators as well as performers in genuine, fulsome, lived encounters with one another across racial and cultural difference. Created by cis-gendered female Inuk artist Laakkuluk Williamson Bathory, and White, queer, settler artist Evalyn Parry, *Kiinalik* modeled a collaboration between Indigenous and settler perspectives that demonstrated how we might take both the land and the lifeways it carries seriously at the theatre, as theatre's "ground"; that is, it demonstrated how we might regard both Indigenous lands and lifeways as central to the workings of "space" at the theatre, in order to support the ongoing struggle for Indigenous sovereign rights in our colonial present.

Locating Settler Colonialism

Before we explore *Kiinalik*, we need a robust understanding of the term "settler colonialism," and we need to understand where we each stand in relation to the term. As Mohawk scholar Audra Simpson writes, "Settler colonialism is predicated on a territorial possession by some and, thus, a dispossession of others" (Simpson 2011: 205). Citing Patrick Wolfe, Simpson notes that the settler-colonial model is one in which the colonizing population "never leaves" and therefore the settler-colonial enterprise requires, ultimately, the disappearance of Indigenous populations in order to be a success (205). "Settlement" in this context means at least two things. First, the term refers to the "settling-in" of the colonial population, for example those who came from Europe to Turtle Island (now known as North America) in the seventeenth through twentieth centuries, a process that included the taking over and clearing of land for farming and city-building, along with the eradication of Indigenous peoples through land dispossession, legal disenfranchisement, and/or cultural assimilation, including via grassroots violence, government-sanctioned violence, as well as the rule of European law (Simpson 2011: 208). Second, the term refers to the "settling-down" of the Indigenous population, who were made after conquest to live in fixed places (on reservation lands, for example, as opposed to freely following traditional hunting cycles), and to take up a fixed, Christian worldview imposed by settler-colonial overlords in place of traditional ceremony and ritual practices (Robinson 2018: 100–4). As Wolfe argues, the "elimination" of Indigenous populations lies at the heart of settler-colonial strategies; however, the proper reason for this elimination is not actually race, religion, or the apparent lack of civility of Indigenous peoples. The reason for elimination is territory: access to land and resources. "Territoriality is settler colonialism's specific, irreducible element," Wolfe notes (2006: 388). Territoriality is a practice of conquest predicated on the sole, private ownership of space, and it is based on the fundamental recognition that space *is never just land*. Space—which as we already know is an idea expansive to its core—means in a settler-colonial context access to and ownership over everything land offers: the fundamentals of social, cultural, and economic power over human populations and their rights of self-determination.

Who, then, is a settler? Are all who are not Indigenous peoples settlers, and therefore complicit in the practices of settler colonialism? Wolfe makes the important assertion that settler colonialism is a structure of power and governance, not a unique, temporally bounded event (it is not here, then over; it is here, potentially forever). White settler scholar Cory Snelgrove takes up this claim and notes that "settlers have to be made and power relations between and among settlers and Indigenous peoples have to be reproduced in order for settler colonialism to extend temporally and spatially" (Snelgrove, Dhamoon, and Corntassel 2014: 5). This reproduction can take active, violent forms (as at first contact), but it can also take the form of routine, passive, barely noticed disavowals of Indigenous claims to rights, land, and sovereignty. As Snelgrove writes, situating himself as a settler in the conversation he curates with Cherokee scholar Corntassel and Sikh scholar Dhamoon, "if we do not want to, my family and I do not have to think about, let alone experience, the violent processes that condition(ed) how we came and come to be here" (5). Writing from the perspective of an immigrant settler woman of color, Dhamoon adds, “Settler colonialism does not work at the individual level, or need my consent or the consent of other individuals even, for it is a way of governing through a naturalized nation-state that erases Indigenous peoples and implicates us all, however well-intentioned we are, or differentially located” (7).

Settlers, Snelgrove and Dhamoon remind us, are made and remade performatively, in our most basic quotidian practices: in the ways we move through familiar spaces whose historical owners we passively ignore; in the ways we daily fail to account for the rights of the historical guardians of the lands we enjoy as public (out and about in the city) or even private (our very homes, the lands they sit upon). Settler status is guaranteed by our most ordinary relationships to space; similarly, however, the ordinarily toxic relationship between settler and Indigenous populations may be disrupted by a willing reorientation, a different orientation *in space*, toward the lands we occupy and the others who lay fair claim to it. Snelgrove, Dhamoon, and Corntassel write that “solidarity between Indigenous and non-Indigenous peoples must be grounded in actual practices and place-based relationships, and be approached as incommensurable but not incompatible” (2014: 3) in order for such a reorientation to become possible. Robinson adds, “as an everyday form of political activism ... identifying as a settler subject marks oneself as possessing a certain awareness of the ongoing inequities faced by Indigenous peoples”; at the same time, he argues, the term “settler” deserves expansion and precision in order to clarify how each non-Indigenous inhabitant of a colonized place is oriented in space toward Indigenous populations, and in order to guard against the performance of “a certain righteousness ... without necessarily contending with one’s individual responsibilities and commitments in the larger project of decolonization” (2018: 94).

Above, I referred to myself as a White settler. I am the child of German immigrants who arrived in Canada in the late 1950s, and who were themselves displaced persons during the Second World War. They were refugees in their homeland, but they came to Canada freely for the opportunities it afforded, taking advantage of the possibilities of good jobs, home ownership, and access to other middle-class resources more easily procured here than in postwar Europe. After studying in Canada and then in Britain I returned to Ontario for my doctoral studies, because I was offered Canadian government funding to pursue my research; I subsequently took a job, bought a house, and established my own middle-class life in Southern Ontario. I was born in a suburb of Montreal, on the lands of the Haudenosauneega, Huron-Wendat, Kanien'kehá:ka, and Mohawk nations; I grew up in Edmonton, on the lands of the Métis, Tsuu T'ina, and Nēhiyawēwin nations. Today I work in London, Ontario, on the lands of the Anishinaabe, Haudenosaunee, Lunaapeewak, and Attawandaron peoples.[2]

In the introduction to this book, as I was describing the ways in which space can be astonishingly abstract, seemingly impossible to grasp, I referenced briefly the practices of colonial conquest that often attach to our desires to grab hold of "space" (p. 14). I then noted how local, granular, and individualized space can become when we need it to help us define, orient, and actualize our very senses of self, and to do that I described the room in which I was writing—my place, my space. That room is in the house I own, and that house sits on Treaty 3 land (1792, the "Between the Lakes Purchase"). That land belonged to the Anishinaabe and Haudenosaunee peoples; in 1784 approximately 3 million acres were ceded for £1,180 worth of goods, to negotiators acting on behalf of the British Crown, by chiefs representing the Mississaugas of the New Credit nation.[3] I live, and write, and work on treaty land; the space that defines me, who I regard myself to be, *is* treaty land.

Seeing Like a Settler

Not all settlers are created equal: some trace ancestry to the first colonizers of a land, some arrive as economic migrants, and some arrive as refugees. Some are trafficked to this place. Others come for fresh plunder, for real estate deals and stock market opportunities. If settler is a mindset, an orientation toward land on the one hand and Indigenous sovereignty on another, then it is also produced in the ways we look at, react to, and consume Indigenous images, narratives, and experiences. Settlers are often made and remade at the theatre: we can be hailed in the ways we are asked to consume spectacles of "traditional" cultures not our own, and we can be produced through our subsequent acts of consuming those spectacles, as though they were built only for our enjoyment. Decolonizing the spaces of the settler-colonial theatre therefore requires settler audiences to become aware of the assumptions and expectations that we carry with us to performances by Indigenous artists, or to performances made in collaboration with Indigenous artists. It requires us to disrupt our most fundamental understandings of what those performances are staging, of *what* we are seeing, *where* we are seeing, but also *how* we are seeing when we look up at the stage.

In his 2018 book[4] of the same name, Stó:lō musicologist (and Canada Research Chair in Indigenous Arts at Queen's University) Dylan Robinson describes what he terms "hungry listening." Robinson explains:

> From a xwélméxw [Stó:lō] perspective, one predominant form of settler listening (and perception more generally) emerges out of a state of consumption and extraction. This is not a generalization of colonization, but instead is derived from the historical and contemporary relationships Stó:lō people have had with non-Indigenous people in our territories, embedded in the Halq'emeylem word Stó:lō people (xwélméxw) use for non-Indigenous settlers: "xwelítem" (or "xwenitem" in Squamish, Muqeuam, Tsleil-Waututh and other Coast Salish communities). However, the words "xwelítem" and "xwenitem" are much more than the equivalent term for "settler"; more accurately they mean "starving person." (105)

Robinson notes how the experience of first contact between Stó:lo and non-Indigenous White visitors and settlers in what is now British Columbia in the nineteenth century involved literal hunger on the part of the latter: starving for food, they were also starving for the gold, for the resources in the mountains and valleys of the lower Fraser River. "It is an understatement to say that this hunger for resources has not abated with time. Xwelítem [settler] hunger has long existed for the rocks, the trees, the water, and the land itself. Each has been thirsted after, each has been consumed," Robinson writes. He quotes novelist Lee Maracle: "The settlers were a dry riverbed possessing a thirst that was never slacked." Furthermore, Robinson adds, "in the twentieth century the hunger has grown as our knowledge and our artistic practices have also been consumed" (105).

Where does settler hunger for the knowledge, artistry, and cultural practices of Indigenous peoples come from? Partly it comes from the fantasy of "empty" or "untamed" or "free" land, on which North America as we know it today was built; in large measure, however, it comes from the learned, European orientation toward aesthetic beauty, the sense that for something represented to be valuable, it must also be attractive, understandable, and available to be consumed. Robinson notes that Western (i.e., settler-oriented) listening practices, when they encounter soundscapes that emerge from Indigenous traditions and perspectives or from encounters between contemporary Indigenous and "classical" Western art music, can be characterized as hunger for "certain kinds of stories (in the current period of reconciliation stories of trauma, of healing, and transformation); a hunger for palatable cultural expression over explicitly political work; a hunger for friendly forms of coming together over agonistic forms of dialogue; a hunger for that which is recognizably Indigenous over the everyday or urban" (106). Listeners hunger to know, to enjoy a glimpse of what Canadian scholar Daniel Francis in 1992 called "the imaginary Indian"—Indigenous peoples as attractive, exotic, and remarkable.

Robinson also notes a crucial difference between the efficacy of Indigenous music and that of Western music—i.e., between the things these forms are understood *to do*. For settlers trained in European listening traditions, Robinson notes, music's beauty and thus its efficacy lies in "listening for" things like formal structures, solos, and generic music conventions. (If you have taken an Introduction to Musicology or a Music Appreciation class, you will know exactly what this means.) This seeking of specific content *in* the music defines the traditional Euro-Western listening experience, Robinson explains: "Listening for content operates on both the level of familiarity (to feel pleasure from the satisfaction of recognition) and on the level of certainty (that one can pride oneself on finding the content that one should listen for)" (2018: 106).

By contrast, much Indigenous music is powerfully performative, and materially functional: songs and other embodied performances act as legal contracts, oral histories, as well as acts of political intervention, or formal claims to status. To illustrate what this means, Robinson describes a 1985 land claims trial in British Columbia in which "counsel for the plaintiffs directed Mary Johnson, Gitxsan hereditary chief Antgulilibix, to perform a limx'ooy (dirge song) associated with her adaawk (formal ancient collectively owned oral history)" (96). The presiding judge, Justice MacEachern, after expressing a fair amount of skepticism, permitted the performance. When it ended, however, he declared:

> All right Mr. Grant, would you explain to me, because this may happen again, why you think it was necessary to sing the song? This is a trial, not a performance ... It is not necessary in a matter of this kind for that song to have been sung, and I think that I must say now that I ought not to have been exposed to it. I don't think it should happen again. (qtd. in Robinson 2018: 99)

As Robinson concludes, the limx'ooy's function as a legal and historical declaration "operates outside the western conception of song" and was thus fundamentally incomprehensible to MacEachern's settler ears (he claimed, ironically, that the song's performance would ultimately be wasted on him, as he had a "tin ear"). MacEachern was unable to grasp the fact that "Indigenous ontologies of song ask us to re-orient what we think we are listening to, and how we go about our practices of listening with responsibilities to listen differently" (99). It is fair to assume that MacEachern did not believe Indigenous forms of knowing were the equals to Euro-American forms of knowing; it is also reasonable to assume he did not even recognize that Euro-American forms of knowing—and the Euro-American sense of songs as "entertainment"—are not the only way to "know" the world. His settler blindness, his "hungry" listening, left him hungry indeed in this instance, and therefore without the capacity to offer Chief Johnson a fair hearing.

How can we challenge, if not overcome, "hungry" settler listening, both at musical performance and at all forms of embodied performance, including at the theatre? What is needed, Robinson argues, is "a practice of listening that understands [Indigenous, as well as collaborative Indigenous-Western] music not as aesthetic content that can be recognized and then consumed. Instead, we must draw upon Indigenous conceptions of song as more-than-aesthetic to understand musical experience as an auditory space that one enters into" (106). Robinson provocatively terms this entering-into, this auditory space, "sound territories" (106); by this term he means "not solely a land-based model of perception" but rather the act of "developing a different practice of guest listening; or perhaps a call to listen to the interaction between Indigenous and settler sound worlds as models of nation-to-nation negotiation, or of trade" (107). Sound territories are territories of encounter, on equitable terms; they are a renovation of performance space not as "to-be-grabbed" but as to-be-built-upon, across cultures and nations, in and through a recognition of both shared investments and practices, but also indissoluble historical and cultural differences.

Robinson's work in musicology is not directly portable to non-musical theatre contexts, of course, but his notion of "sound territory" shares valuable kinship with other forms of embodied encounter being theorized by Indigenous scholars of theatre and their allies. In a 2015 article, "Discarding Sympathy, Disrupting Catharsis: The Mortification of Indigenous Flesh as Survivance-Intervention," Anishinaabe/Ashkenazi scholar Jill Carter examines contrasting Indigenous performance works "that solicit and elicit a sympathetic response from their witnesses" and weighs the audience outcomes of these works "against performative interventions that reject a sympathetic response and demand from their witnesses empathic, effective action to engender social transformation" (415). In the contrast Carter draws between sympathy and empathy, she parallels the contrast Robinson draws between hungry listening "for" and sustained engagements "with" performers and their practices—on the terms set out by those performers and their worldviews, not on settler terms. Similarly, Carter, co-writing with settler scholars Heather Davis-Fisch and Ric Knowles, develops a theory of Indigenous performance "circulation" in a 2017 article that reconfigures the trajectory of colonial transfers of theatrical knowledge in the modern period. Working against the conventional understanding that Indigenous performers always traveled, figuratively or literally, in order to return to the colonial "center" (e.g., "Indian" performers at World's Fairs or those famously transported to London for royal wonderment and pleasure in the nineteenth century), Carter, Davis-Fisch, and Knowles argue that Indigenous musical, theatre, and other performance forms—and the "more-than-aesthetic" resistance they enact to colonial governance—lie everywhere, often unacknowledged, inside the "Western" art works of the colonial and postcolonial periods in North America.

Like Robinson's transformation of "hungry" listening into a sound-encounter on shared sound-territory, and Carter's understanding of empathy as a practice of lived, risked encounter between settler (as well as Indigenous) spectators and Indigenous performances, Carter, Davis-Fisch, and

Knowles's fresh conception of theatrical circulation requires us to "unsettle" the spatial and temporal structures (from *there* to *here*; from *then* to *now*) by which colonial imaginations typically regard Indigenous others and their cultural processes.[5] In *Unsettling Space*, Joanne Tompkins (who is a White, Canadian-born settler scholar working in Australia) undertakes exactly this project of "unsettlement." She frames her readings of the contested spaces of late twentieth- and early twenty-first-century Australian theatre with the histories of violent settlement on Australian territory. Tompkins, who as we have seen is a leading scholar of theatre studies' "spatial turn," brings theories of space and place directly and forcefully to bear on her landmark readings, and thus provides exemplary evidence of how the spatial turn is already engaging with the fraught but urgent project of theatrical decolonization. In her introduction to *Unsettling Space*, Tompkins writes:

> Debates over land rights, anxieties regarding nationalism, settlement, reconciliation, traces of what was known as the yellow peril and subsequent invasion scares are preoccupied with space. These debates have resulted in the paradoxical depiction of Australia as an unlimited, empty land, at the same time as it is said to be too "full" to accommodate outsiders, such as asylum seekers. These depictions converge in the historical context of settlement, but settlement … gives way to moments of what I call "unsettlement" in the Australian theatre. My use of the term … recognizes that the history of settlement in Australia is both profoundly unstable and the cause of cultural anxiety. (Tompkins 2006: 6)

To listen without hunger; to unsettle and confront the "cultural anxiety" that shapes the spaces of our theatrical viewing. To encounter art works made by others, in their proper otherness, and on the very different terms provided by their unique ontologies (modes of being and understanding), as well as by their violent but also enduring histories. To engage with the actions those performances undertake, beyond aesthetics or entertainment. To hear their demands for sovereignty, for human rights. These are incredibly worthy goals, but also extraordinary audience challenges. How can they be accomplished, practically? In my final pages, I'll offer some thoughts on my own recent unsettlement, my own labor of listening beyond hunger, at *Kiinalik: These Sharp Tools* (2017). It is only one of dozens of recent, provocative, Indigenous-led theatre works I could have chosen to close this book.[6]

"A Concert and a Conversation": *Kiinalik: These Sharp Tools*

Before the show begins, director Erin Brubacher comes to the edge of the stage and says, "Hello everyone." She announces that she will be audio-describing the performance by co-creators Laakkuluk Williamson Bathory and Evalyn Parry, and musician Cris Derksen, and encourages us to return to talking amongst ourselves before they take the stage.

Brubacher offers a broad, inclusive welcome: an invitation to conversation with one another, a reminder not to assume normative bodies in the audience or on stage, and an emphasis on the aural, performative, and embodied—as well as the shared, the co-created—over the solo, virtuosic, or the purely textual. Hers is an act of recognition: it makes us visible and audible to each other. It also makes visible the multiple forms of practice, of understanding

Parts of my discussion of *Kiinalik* are adapted from "'These Sharp Tools': Coming to Terms, or The Squeezebox," a reflection on the play I co-authored with So Mayer. I've placed these portions of the text in italics. I'm grateful to Mayer for permission to offer text from our shared work here.

> *and experiencing the world—hearing and speaking with ears and with hands; singing and sharing from the stage and in the auditorium; encountering one another in our shared human-ness, but also in our difference—that will be normative throughout the show. Her announcement gives us, informally but importantly, a tool to understand that* Kiinalik, *devised and written by Williamson Bathory (Inuk, straight) and Parry (settler, queer), will be above all a work of listening.*

This opening announcement—which is also an opening out, a moving comfortably across the stage/auditorium boundary, something else that will be typical throughout the performance to come—carries its spirit directly into the first part of *Kiinalik: These Sharp Tools*. Parry and Williamson Bathory (who refer to one another on stage as Evalyn and Laakkuluk) step up to separate microphones, in front of a backdrop of video screens. They are physically separated by the space between their mic stands, but they orient their bodies, turn their heads and torsos, toward one another constantly. They are very aware of what separates them. They are also very aware of wanting to come together. They do not pretend either of these things is easy—even though they have become close friends in the making of this work.[7]

Laakkuluk's mic is also a space with a difference, because magnetized to it is an ulu, a traditional, half-moon-shaped, Inuk carving knife. It is her knife; she uses it all the time, in her art-making as well as in her cooking and other daily tasks. It is a tool of representation, a tool of laboring, a survival tool, a quotidian tool. It is an everyday object that makes space, in this particular performance space, for Laakkuluk's lived, embodied difference, her lived distance from Evalyn and from many of us in the audience. It asks us to listen, keenly, to her difference, to recognize, and respect, and account for, and witness it.

Laakkuluk and Evalyn begin the show by telling us something of how they met. They were on a boat, in the Arctic—an "exploration" vessel, a science ship. Laakkuluk was there as a kind of cultural ambassador and instructor; she was one of a tiny handful of Inuk aboard, there to accommodate visitors' quests for knowledge about Inuk lifeways (their well-meaning but still hungry listening). Parry was on board to learn, too; she found the journey challenging, though. She describes her seasickness to us early in the show. A folk singer, Evalyn plays guitar and squeezebox and contributes sung testimony, along with Laakkuluk, throughout the performance. Here, she sings of her seasickness as a disorder that occurs "when your eyes can't see what your body is feeling." Seasickness is embodied displacement; body and brain are out-of-space with each other. The cure, she tells us, is to step on deck and find the horizon: to face the overwhelming vastness of the ocean, see the through-line, realign. As they met, talked, and faced the ocean together, Evalyn and Laakkuluk discovered how much they actually had in common.

They met on a boat; this matters to the story. A boat may seem, to settler imaginations, not of the land—not contested territory. From an Indigenous worldview, an Inuk worldview, though, this is not true. Water is part of the land: it is part of the hunting, fishing, cultural, historical, lived, and memoried grounds of a people. It is survivance space, as Vizenor and Carter would say. And it is contested space—otherwise, that Arctic vessel, that Canadian government ship, would not be out there, hunting for something.

> *Writing together about the show, later, So [Mayer] and I go over the stories Evalyn and Laakkuluk tell us about their initial encounters. The show reveals bits and pieces about them, individually and together: they are both "laughers" and "criers," both married, both with British fathers, both with dead fathers. They met on a boat, "touring" the Arctic. (A boat that carried exponentially more scientists than it did Inuk.) But the origin of their story, we soon realize, remains missing; the bit that they keep to themselves is that loaded moment of "first contact," the dead-centre moment. Ground zero. The fetish moment of all settler-colonial narratives, the encounter usually rendered, frozen, in art: this is theirs alone, not for our hungry ears and eyes.*

After sharing brief snapshots of their pasts, Evalyn and Laakkuluk sing together the Skye Boat Song. They tell us it was sung to them both as babies; it is a shared history. A birthright between them. The Skye Boat Song comes from the Highland Clearances; it is a reminder that the British Isles are also a land alive with strong memories of settler colonialism. And, as it invokes the worlds of the Hebrides—closer to Norway than to London—the song is a reminder of a shared circumpolar culture, an alternate spatial framework (round, not vertical; from above, not from the "West" or the "North") for recognizing and ordering our earth.

The Skye Boat Song is an offer to the audience as well, an invitation into a shared cultural practice most, if not all, spectators at this particular theatre will know. But it's an offer with a twist. At this point in the performance, Evalyn and Laakkuluk ask their technical team to bring up the house lights; then they turn to us. Where is the furtherest north we've been? They ask. Or the furthest place north to which we are connected? They ask us to turn to the people near us—on either side and in front and behind, not just on one side—and answer these questions. Introduce ourselves. Share our previous journeys.

The set of *Kiinalik*'s stage is fully collaborative: the two white video screens at center stage are angled toward each other, just as Laakkuluk and Evalyn angle themselves toward one another. Cris's instruments and musical tools lie about, comfortably, to stage right, where she also sits and works in full audience view; Evalyn's guitar and squeezebox, and her loop pedals, sit nearby. At this point in the performance, though, I realize it's not just the stage, but the whole theatre space—auditorium too—that has been designed to seem entirely collaborative: the floor is painted to appear like ice, and ice fills the lip of the stage. We are connected to the performers, and they to us, by this ice: by the land on which Evalyn and Laakkuluk met, the land of Inuk, circumpolar land. We are not "of" their space, strictly speaking—we sit in the auditorium, in a traditional rake, in a space that marks us plainly as different from those telling this story—but we are still a part of the story's larger space, the space of its reverberations. And, at this moment in the story, we are explicitly invited to join in.

Evalyn and Laakkuluk call us back together after about five minutes; they ask to hear about our conversations. As people feed in, Laakkuluk asks Elysha Poirier, the show's videographer seated in the technical booth at the back of the audience, to scroll up and down on a live map of the earth on the stage's video screens. Together, Laakkuluk and Elysha find on the map the places we have traveled. We scroll far north of the usual "global" place-holders (New York, London, Toronto) that orient us on conventional, Western maps—the maps where Europe and North America appear far larger than they physically are, because racial and cultural perception makes space, remember. We zoom in on Laakkuluk's home in Iqualuit. We zoom in on the islands to the north. We scroll across the North Pole to northern Russia. We see our earth from the top down. We laugh at coincidences—one guy has been to an outport in Nunavut, a place where Laakkuluk has family. We refer to each other in the audience by name. We watch Elysha strive to locate tiny, tiny villages on the huge, "global" map. We help her. We take real, shared pleasure, but we are also dis-oriented by this atypical map-play.

Not long after this moment in the show passes, Laakkuluk brings an overhead projector on stage. She pulls it through the aisle in between the banks of our seats, and she stands with it in the space between stage and audience. She has nothing to show us; this is not a moment of representation. Rather, it is a moment of creation. She tells us the stories of her tattoos, those that encircle her arms and legs. She tells us how the women of her nation were shamed by colonizers, by missionaries and others, for adorning their bodies. As she talks she carves fresh tattoos into the acetate on the projector with the point of her ulu; we see the tattoos emerge as lines of light on the screen behind us. She explains how the tattoos are history, women's history, Inuk history, carried on her body as ancestry: they are not images, but enactments. They are lived, living memory;

they are not for "show" (and not for us). As the fresh acetate carvings appear above and behind her on the screens they make Laakkuluk's body appear large, strong, many bodies at once; this hybrid body, full of dense design, art, and history, takes up the whole space of the stage by the end of her monologue. She inhabits that space with force and ease. She conquers it, takes it back.

Next, Laakkuluk pulls paints and tools from a drawer below the projector. She paints her face with black and red makeup, and inserts two small balls into her cheeks, puffing them out, transforming her face into a strange smile. Laakkuluk changes in this way into one of her ancestors, a hungry ancestor. (A hungry ancestor is very different from a hungry settler; a hungry ancestor is the product of forced Indigenous displacement, dispossession, and disorientation [Carter 2015].) Laakkuluk now moves into the crowd as she performs an Uajeerneq, a Greenlandic dance, in which she is a particular specialist. She groans and grunts, the sounds strong in her throat—the roar of a truly hungry body. She is sexual, explicit; as she climbs over spectators' limbs and torsos to reach the next tier of seats she lands in laps, grinds against us, breathes into our faces. She steals the notebooks of the students in the crowd (some of my students lose theirs, or have their notes smudged by paint). She smiles that ball smile, a wicked, urgent smile—a smile full of urges, not "civilized" urges. She is in *our* space, the space of our hungry and sympathetic watching, and she is way, way too close to us. She is not respecting our personal space. It seems the creature she has become does not understand Western conceptions of "personal space" at all—maybe just like Justice MacEachern did not understand Indigenous song as history, as a claim under the law. But with a difference.

Laakkuluk does not climb onto me. I am both a bit relieved and quite disappointed by this. In my disappointment I recognize my hungry listening, needful watching: I want to *have* this experience, want to know what it is like to feel Laakkuluk's body on top of mine. I feel suddenly a bit like a tourist. Ashamed, I try to channel my viewing differently.

I try to observe how others are observing and reacting to Laakkuluk's dancing body, her ritual movements, her stolen freedom-of-place. Some look utterly delighted, are laughing. (A lot of men react this way, I notice.) Some wear poker faces; I can see them reacting the way they think they "ought" to react. (I would do this too, I observe.) Some are stony-faced, even panicked. One woman looks as though she has left her body altogether, forced out of consciousness by sheer terror. Two other spectators stand to leave the theatre; I notice there are staffers planted in the audience to support those who need to get away. (One, I notice now, is seated next to me.) This is a difficult, challenging, deeply uncomfortable sequence in the performance, and it is going on for a very, very long time. But it is not meant to be hurtful. It is meant to be a process of learning, or perhaps unlearning. Laakkuluk is challenging our viewing—our *points of view*; our viewing as a space-making technology—directly, with her body. She is challenging the meaning of the space between her body and ours, the space that hungry listeners seem to want to collapse as they collect the sounds and art and artifacts of Indigenous performers for themselves. She is challenging where we think we are—whose place, whose home, we believe we are in. She is challenging what we think this performance is "for," what we think this performance *is*. And for whom we think this performance is, too.

Later, I debrief with my students. They ask me if the Uajeerneq should have come with a trigger warning; after all, it obviously unsettled (literally) some people very deeply. I tell them I don't know. On the one hand, Laakkuluk is narrating a history of cultural genocide, the forced displacement of her nation, their deprivation under colonialism; do we really have the right, then, as we sit comfortably in our seats, not to feel uncomfortable, unsettled, by her dance? On the other hand, the reactions of some spectators indicate that, clearly, Laakkuluk's invasion of "our" theatrical space was more than a public and political act, more than *her* personal act of spatial reclamation. It intersected in ways unknown with others' experiences of space, of displacement, of dispossession. One of my students, a Syrian refugee who sought asylum in Canada in 2016, tells me she will never be able to forget the Uajeerneq, because it left her deeply scarred. I realize that neither I nor Laakkuluk could know what she, herself, went through to get from Syria to here. Where her new boundaries lie, or what this space we share means to her.

I remember that settlement is a process, not an event. That settlers are made, and not made equally. That settler experiences encounter Indigenous experiences in their own deep differences. The spaces between us are not empty, not clear.

> *Uajeerneq is a performance action in space; it is also a process through which Laakkuluk invites her witnesses to become vulnerable with her, powerful with her, playful with her, uncomfortable in a fraught, shared space—the space of settler-colonization, perhaps—with her. It is one of* Kiinalik*'s many performative strategies for decolonization, for which there are perhaps not yet good English terms. Laakkuluk reminds us that names are not just words, but souls. Some things we can't just talk about, so easily. That does not mean that they are not present, not urgent, not real.*
>
> Kiinalik *is described in its promotional materials as "a concert and a conversation," but it is only a beginning. More listening, not hungry listening, is needed before settler audiences have the sharp tools that Laakkuluk wields so powerfully, the responsive listening that Evalyn wields so gently. Before those of us from settler backgrounds can fully understand how Laakkuluk's tattoos are not "symbols" for each other, but kin: relations. Before we can acknowledge the accountability of our own looking relations, across time and across space.*

NOTES

Introduction

1 The relationship between the linked terms "place" and "space" is contested. "Place" is often used to denote the local, or the idea of being located in a specific site with clear particularities, while "space" is typically the larger, more abstract marker. (There are limits to this generalization, as to all generalizations, but throughout this book I will use these two connotations unless otherwise noted.) This does not mean "space" and "place" perform in fixed binary relation to each other, however; as Arnold Aronson suggests (2013: 88), citing de Certeau's notion of space as "practiced place" (1984: 117), theatre buildings are lived "places" that become "space" when we erect dramatic worlds upon their stages. In other words, the deeper into a theatrical world we travel, the more expansive its spatial dimensions become. I'll speak more about theatre's particular brand of spatial expansiveness in the first section; meanwhile, for more on "place" in the history of human thought, see Casey, *The Fate of Place: A Philosophical History.*

2 For an extended reading of Morahan's work in this production, see Solga, *Theatre & Feminism.*

3 And after Lefebvre, Edward Soja and Doreen Massey (among others), both influential in their own right. I will discuss this strand of human geography in the first section.

Section One

1 As this book is focused largely on the long twentieth century, this short historical foray will necessarily be partial; it will also not include a history of performance spaces. For those interested in

such a history, two excellent starting points are Wiles, *A Short History of Western Performance Space* ([2003] 2007), and the chapters focused on space (one per volume) in the six-volume *A Cultural History of Theatre* (Balme and Davis 2017).

2 By "conservative" here I mean the generic sense of conserving existing belief systems, ontological frameworks, and status quos; I am not referring to a specific political affiliation. When invested in the social status quo, for example, "liberals" can be thought of as conservative.

3 For much more on the impact of Heidegger on the structure of social space see Levin 2014, chapter 1.

4 Harvie's own cultural materialist influences include the philosopher Raymond Williams and the performance theorist Ric Knowles, especially Knowles's influential 2004 book, *Reading the Material Theatre*.

5 In fact, Bayreuth and the two Stratfords all qualify as small cities by at least some standards. Bayreuth had a population of 72,148 in 2015; Stratford-upon-Avon is classified as a "market town" (or regional hub) and had a population of 27,445 in 2011; Stratford, Ontario, by contrast, is called a "city" on its Wikipedia page, with a population of 31,465 in 2016. Some of the confusion around terminology here stems from the fact that the steady, increasingly rapid urbanization of our planet is also steadily changing the way we talk about who we live with, and where we live. See Solga 2009: 1, as well as Saunders 2010.

6 Austin uses the example of the wedding ceremony as a clear performative utterance: when the officiant (a priest or municipal officer) pronounces a couple husband and wife, or wife and wife, or husband and husband, those words *literally* change the legal status of two individuals. Butler, whose interest lies in the performative nature of gender and sexuality, uses the example of a child's birth: when a doctor announces "it's a girl" or "it's a boy" (1993: 232) that doctor genders the child socially for the first time, setting up all future identifications.

7 The collision of cultural materialism and performance studies methodologies in urban theatre and performance scholarship has been noted and very well explained by Jen Harvie in *Theatre & The City* (2009). There, Harvie also usefully demonstrates

what a blended approach might offer to scholars and students of performance in the city.

8 Nicholas Whybrow's *Performance and the Contemporary City* (2010) is a wide-ranging resource for exploring performance studies methodologies in relation to urban performance. It includes sections on walking, drifting, sound and rhythm, play and gaming, among other things. See also Hopkins, Orr, and Solga, *Performance and the City* (2009).

9 Note that Strindberg had moved beyond naturalism when the Intima was founded in 1907, though his naturalist works were among the theatre's most successful productions.

10 While Turner's book is interested in "theatre as a spatial art" (155–85) primarily in the time and place of Shakespeare and his contemporaries, his interdisciplinary analysis provides an excellent example of how critical work from outside a specific research context can nevertheless lend fresh nuance and perspective to that context.

11 Contemporary scenography is similarly interested in the special embodied nature of theatrical space, taking a design-forward perspective. See for example Aronson 2018 and Shepherd 2005.

12 This may be one reason why Garner (citing Bert States) calls phenomenology and semiotics "complementary ways of seeing that disclose the object in two ways at once" (1994: 15). They can similarly reveal two different aspects of stage space: its symbolic, signifying capacity, and its material, embodied elements.

13 Garner's chapter on Samuel Beckett and the image-theatre tradition in modernism in fact precedes his chapter on realism and naturalism; it is central to his articulation of the tension between the pictorial and the embodied in contemporary dramatic space.

Section Two

1 The archive video of *Fräulein Julie* is available for purchase at minimal cost from the Schaubühne Berlin. The work remains in the theatre's cyclical repertoire.

2 *The Shipment* is available to watch free of charge on Young Jean Lee's Theatre Company website (http://youngjeanlee.org/work/the-shipment/). In this section, I'll be referencing moments from this video, by minute and second mark. A full list of creative team members, as well as photos and press, is available on the website as well.

3 For more on the minstrel show in American popular culture, see Eric Lott's *Love and Theft: Blackface Minstrelsy and the American Working Class* (1995), and *Inside the Minstrel Mask*, edited by Bean, Hatch, and McNamara (1996).

4 This line comes from Massey 2007: 10.

5 The sunken place is a reference to Jordan Peele's 2017 film, *Get Out*. The film is a dark mirror of *The Shipment*, and well worth a viewing.

Section Three

1 My discussion in this final section is based in part on my experience as a resident of Turtle Island, or North America, and specifically of the colonial nation of Canada. It is, however, applicable to practices in nations around the world where Indigenous populations remain without access to their full land or human rights. For an excellent introduction to the contexts and politics of settler-colonial Canada, see Lowman and Barker 2015.

2 The website https://native-land.ca helped me determine precisely on whose land I work and live. It is an independently funded work in progress and relies on user input to continually refine its territory information.

3 Read more about the MNCFN on their community website, including much more about the history of Treaty 3: http://mncfn.ca/.

4 I am quoting a pre-publication edition of Robinson's book; at the time of this writing it is not yet commercially available. Pagination for the quotations below may vary in the published edition.

5 Knowles (along with Algonquin/Irish playwright and director Yvette Nolan) is also co-editor of (and both Carter and Robinson are contributors to) the important collection of essays and

reflections by Indigenous scholars and artists, *Performing Indigeneity* (2016). It is a terrific introduction to what it might mean to enact sovereignty over theatre, performance, and its social labor from an Indigenous North American perspective.

6 Others (only a handful!) include *Chocolate Woman Dreams the Milky Way*, by Monique Mojica; *Huff*, by Cliff Cardinal (discussed eloquently by Carter in her 2015 article); *Making Treaty 7—We Are All Treaty People*, by the Treaty 7 Cultural Society (see resources on this volume's companion website); and *Reckoning*, by Article 11 theatre (Tara Beagan and Andy Moro).

7 For a felt sense of what this performance looked like, see the show's visual story, available online at http://buddiesinbadtimes.com/wp-content/uploads/Visual-Story-Kiinalik-These-Sharp-Tools.pdf (or click the link available on this volume's companion website).

REFERENCES

Ahmed, S. (2004), *The Cultural Politics of Emotion*, London: Routledge.

And While London Burns (2007), Dir. J. Jordan and J. Marriott, Platform, London.

Aristotle ([c. 335BC] 2000), "Poetics," in D. Gerould (ed.), *Theatre / Theory / Theatre: The Major Critical Texts from Aristotle and Zeami to Soyinka and Havel*, New York: Applause Theatre and Cinema Books.

Aronson, A. (2013), "Time and Space on the Stage," *Performance Research* 18 (3): 84–94.

Aronson, A. (2018), *The History and Theory of Environmental Scenography*, 2nd ed., London: Methuen Drama.

Balme, C. B. (2014), *The Theatrical Public Sphere*, Cambridge: Cambridge University Press.

Balme, C. B. and T. Davis, eds. (2017), *A Cultural History of Theatre*, 6 vols., London: Bloomsbury.

Barker, R., K. Solga, and C. Mazer (2013), "'Tis Pity She's a Realist: A Conversational Case Study in Realism and Early Modern Theater Today," *Shakespeare Bulletin*, 31 (4): 571–97.

Bean, A., J. V. Hatch, and B. McNamara, eds. (1996), *Inside the Minstrel Mask: Readings in Nineteenth-Century Blackface Minstrelsy*, Hanover: University Press of New England.

Bennett, S. (2005), "Theatre/Tourism," *Theatre Journal* 57 (3), October: 407–28.

Bennett, S. (2013), *Theatre & Museums*, Basingstoke: Palgrave Macmillan.

Benjamin, W. (1999), *The Arcades Project*, trans. H. Eiland and K. McLaughlin, ed. R. Tiedemann, Cambridge, MA: Harvard University Press.

Birch, A. and J. Tompkins, eds. (2012), *Performing Site-Specific Theatre: Politics, Place, Practice*, Basingstoke: Palgrave Macmillan.

Borch, C. (2002), "Interview with Edward W. Soja: Thirdspace, Postmetropolis, and Social Theory," *Distinkinktion: Scandinavian Journal of Social Theory*, 3 (1): 113–20.

Borough Market (2018), March 2. http://boroughmarket.org.uk/

Butler, J. (1993), *Bodies That Matter: On the Discursive Limits of "Sex,"* New York: Routledge.

Carlson, Marvin (1989), *Places of Performance: The Semiotics of Theatre Architecture*, Ithaca, NY: Cornell University Press.

Carlson, Marvin (1993), *Theories of the Theatre: A Historical and Critical Survey from the Greeks to the Present*, Ithaca, NY: Cornell University Press.

Carlson, Marvin (2001), *The Haunted Stage: The Theatre as Memory Machine*, Ann Arbor, MI: University of Michigan Press.

Carlson, Marla ([2006] 2009), "Ways to Walk New York after 9/11," in D. J. Hopkins, S. Orr, and K. Solga (eds.), *Performance and the City*, 15–32, Basingstoke: Palgrave Macmillan.

Carnicke, S. (2008), *Stanislavsky in Focus*, 2nd ed., London: Routledge.

Carter, J. (2015), "Discarding Sympathy, Disrupting Catharsis: The Mortification of Indigenous Flesh as Survivance-Intervention," *Theatre Journal*, 67 (3): 413–32.

Carter, J., H. Davis-Fisch, and R. Knowles (2017), "Circulations: Visual Sovereignty, Transmotion, and Tribalography," in K. Solga (ed.), *A Cultural History of Theatre in the Modern Age*, 95–116, London: Bloomsbury.

Casey, E. (1997), *The Fate of Place: A Philosophical History*, Berkeley, CA: University of California Press.

Chaudhuri, U. (1995), *Staging Place: The Geography of Modern Drama*, Ann Arbor, MI: University of Michigan Press.

Cheek By Jowl (2008), "ARTE Documentary on Cheek by Jowl's Cymbeline PART 2," France: ZADIG Productions.

Corneille, P. ([1660] 2000), "Of the Three Unities," in D. Gerould (ed.), *Theatre / Theory / Theatre: The Major Critical Texts from Aristotle and Zeami to Soyinka and Havel*, New York: Applause Theatre and Cinema Books.

De Certeau, M. (1984), *The Practice of Everyday Life*, ed. S. Rendall, Berkeley, CA: University of California Press.

De Vega, L. ([1609] 2000), "The New Art of Writing Plays," in D. Gerould (ed.), *Theatre / Theory / Theatre: The Major Critical Texts from Aristotle and Zeami to Soyinka and Havel*, New York: Applause Theatre and Cinema Books.

Debord, G. (1967), *La Société du Spectacle*, Paris: Buchet Chastel.
Diamond, E. (1997), *Unmaking Mimesis: Essays on Feminism and Theater*, New York: Routledge.
Diamond, E. (2001), "Modern Drama/Modernity's Drama," *Modern Drama*, 44 (1): 3–15.
A Doll's House (2012), Dir. C. Cracknell, The Young Vic, London.
Fischer-Lichte, E. (1992), *The Semiotics of Theatre*, trans. J. Gaines and D. L. Jones, Bloomington, IN: Indiana University Press.
Fischer-Lichte, E. and B. Whistutz, eds. (2012), *Performance and the Politics of Space*, New York: Routledge.
Florida, R. (2002), *The Rise of the Creative Class and How It's Transforming Work, Leisure, Community and Everyday Life*, New York: Basic Books.
Foucault, M. ([1967] 1986), "Of Other Spaces: Utopias and Heterotopias," trans. Jay Miskowiec, *Diacritics*, 16 (1): 22–7.
Fowler, B. (2017), "(Re)mediating the Modernist Novel: Katie Mitchell's Live Cinema Work," in K. Reilly (ed.), *Contemporary Approaches to Adaptation*, 97–119, Basingstoke: Palgrave Macmillan.
Francis, D. (1992), *The Imaginary Indian: The Image of the Indian in Canadian Culture*, Vancouver: Arsenal Pulp Press.
Fräulein Julie (2010), Dir. K. Mitchell, Schaubühne, Berlin.
Garner, S. (1994), *Bodied Spaces: Phenomenology and Performance in Contemporary Drama*, Ithaca, NY: Cornell University Press.
Garner, S. (2008), "Introduction: Is There a Doctor in the House? Medicine and the Making of Modern Drama," *Modern Drama*, 51 (3): 311–28.
Gerould, D., ed. (2000), *Theatre / Theory / Theatre: The Major Critical Texts from Aristotle and Zeami to Soyinka and Havel*, New York: Applause Theatre and Cinema Books.
Gobert, R. D. (2013), *The Mind-Body Stage: Passion and Interaction in the Cartesian Theatre*, Stanford, CA: Stanford University Press.
Harvie, J. (2009), *Theatre & The City*, Basingstoke: Palgrave Macmillan.
Harvie, J. (2013), *Fair Play: Art, Performance and Neoliberalism*, Basingstoke: Palgrave Macmillan.
Hopkins, D. J., S. Orr, and K. Solga, eds. (2009), *Performance and the City*, Basingstoke: Palgrave Macmillan.
Kaye, N. (2000), *Site-Specific Art: Performance, Place, and Documentation*, New York: Routledge.

Kiinalik: These Sharp Tools (2017), Created by E. Parry and L. Williamson Bathory, Buddies in Bad Times Theatre, Toronto.
Kirschenblatt-Gimblett, B. (2002), "Performance Studies," in H. Bial (ed.), *The Performance Studies Reader*, 3rd ed., 43–56, New York: Routledge.
Knowles, R. (2004), *Reading the Material Theatre*, Cambridge: Cambridge University Press.
Knowles, R. (2017), *Performing the Intercultural City*, Ann Arbor, MI: University of Michigan Press.
Knowles, R. and Y. Nolan, eds. (2016), *Performing Indigeneity*, Toronto: Playwrights Canada.
Kucheva, V. (2013), "Scenography at Home," *Performance Research*, 18 (3): 1–2.
Lefebvre, H. ([1974] 1991), *The Production of Space*, trans. D. Nicholson-Smith, Oxford: Blackwell.
Lee, Y. J. (2009), "The Shipment," *Young Jean Lee's Theatre Company Archive*, March 2, 2018. http://youngjeanlee.org.
Levin, L. (2009), "Can the City Speak," in D. J. Hopkins, S. Orr, and K. Solga (eds), *Performance and the City*, 240–57, Basingstoke: Palgrave Macmillan.
Levin, L. (2014), *Performing Ground: Space, Camouflage and the Art of Blending in*, Basingstoke: Palgrave Macmillan.
Levin, L. and K. Solga (2009), "Building Utopia: Performance and Fantasy of Urban Renewal in Contemporary Toronto," *The Drama Review*, 53 (3): 37–53.
London Mithraeum (2018), Bloomberg Space, March 2, 2018, https://www.londonmithraeum.com/
Lotker, S. and R. Gough (2013), "On Scenography: Editorial," *Performance Research* 18 (3): 3–6.
Lott, E. (1995), *Love and Theft: Blackface Minstrelsy and the American Working Class*, New York: Oxford University Press.
Lowman, E. B. and A. J. Barker (2015), *Settler: Identity and Colonialism in 21st Century Canada*, Winnipeg: Fernwood Publishing.
Massey, D. (1994), *Space, Place, and Gender*, Minneapolis, MN: University of Minnesota Press.
Massey, D. (2005), *For Space*, London: SAGE.
Massey, D. (2007), *World City*, Cambridge: Polity Press.
Mayer, S. and K. Solga (2018), "'These Sharp Tools:' Coming to Terms, or The Squeezebox," *Stratford Festival Reviews*, March 2.

https://stratfordfestivalreviews.com/blog/2018/01/14/kiinalik-these-sharp-tools/
McAuley, G. (1999), *Space in Performance: Making Meaning in the Theatre*, Ann Arbor, MI: University of Michigan Press.
McKinnie, M. (2007), *City Stages: Theatre and Urban Space in a Global City*, Toronto: University of Toronto Press.
McKinnie, M. (2009), "Performance the Civic Transnational: Cultural Production, Governance, and Citizenship in Contemporary London," in D. J. Hopkins, S. Orr, and K. Solga (eds.), *Performance and the City*, 110–27, Basingstoke: Palgrave Macmillan.
McKinnie, M. (2017), "Institutional Frameworks: Theatre, State, and Market in Modern Urban Performance," in K. Solga (ed.), *A Cultural History of Theatre in the Modern Age*, 17–33, London: Bloomsbury.
Mississaugas of the New Credit First Nation (2018), March 2, http://mncfn.ca/
Morash, C. and S. Richards (2013), *Mapping Irish Theatre: Theories of Space and Place*, Cambridge: Cambridge University Press.
Nield, S. (2012), "Siting the People: Power, Protest, and Public Space," in A. Birch and J. Tompkins (eds.), *Performing Site-Specific Theatre: Politics, Place, Practice*, 219–33, Basingstoke: Palgrave Macmillan.
Pearson, M. (2010), *Site-Specific Performance*, Basingstoke: Palgrave.
Pearson, M. (2012), "Haunted House: Staging the Persians with the British Army," in A. Birch and J. Tompkins (eds.), *Performing Site-Specific Theatre: Politics, Place, Practice*, 69–84, Basingstoke: Palgrave Macmillan.
Pearson, M. and M. Shanks (2001), *Theatre/Archeology*, New York: Routledge.
Peck, J. (2005), "Struggling with the Creative Class," *International Journal of Urban and Regional Research*, 29 (4): 740–70.
Phelan, P. (1993), *Unmarked: The Politics of Performance*, London: Routledge.
Phelan, P. (1997), *Mourning Sex: Performing Public Memories*, New York: Routledge.
Platformlondon (2018), "About Us," August 27, http://platformlondon.org/about-us/
Rayner, A. (2006), *Ghosts: Death's Double and the Phenomena of Theatre*, Minneapolis, MN: University of Minnesota Press.

Roach, J. (1996), *Cities of the Dead: Circum-Atlantic Performance*, New York: Columbia University Press.

Robinson, D. (2018), *Hungry Listening: Between Indigenous Song and Classical Music*, Minneapolis, MN: University of Minnesota Press (Forthcoming).

Saunders, D. (2010), *Arrival City: The Final Migration and Our Next World*, Toronto: Alfred A. Knopf.

Schechner, R. (1973), *Environmental Theatre*, New York: Hawthorn Books.

Schechner, R. (2002), "Performance Studies: The Broad Spectrum Approach," in H. Bial (ed.), *The Performance Studies Reader*, 3rd ed., 7–10, New York: Routledge.

Schneider, R. (2011), *Performing Remains: Art and War in Times of Theatrical Reenactment*, New York: Routledge.

Shepherd, S. (2005), *Theatre, Body and Pleasure*, London: Routledge.

Shevtsova, M. (2006), "On Directing: A Conversation with Katie Mitchell," *New Theatre Quarterly*, 22 (1): 3–18.

The Shipment (2009), Dir. Y. J. Lee, The Kitchen, New York.

Simpson, A. (2011), "Settlement's Secret," *Cultural Anthropology*, 26 (2): 205–17.

Singer, B. (2001), *Melodrama and Modernity: Early Sensational Cinema and Its Contexts*, New York: Columbia University Press.

Snelgrove, C., R. K. Dhamoon and J. Corntassel (2014), "Unsettling Settler Colonialism: The Discourse and Politics of Settlers, and Solidarity with Indigenous Nations," *Decolonization: Indigeneity, Education and Society*, 3 (2): 1–32.

Soja, E. (1989), *Postmodern Geographies: The Reassertion of Space in Critical Social Theory*, London and New York: Verso.

Soja, E. (1996), *Thirdspace: Journeys to Los Angeles and Other Real and Imagined Places*, Cambridge: Blackwell.

Solga, K. (2009), "City/Text/Performance," in D. J. Hopkins, S. Orr, and K. Solga (eds.), *Performance and the City*, 1–9, Basingstoke: Palgrave Macmillan.

Solga, K. (2016), *Theatre & Feminism*, New York: Palgrave Macmillan.

Solga, K. and J. Tompkins (2017), "Environments of Theatre in the Modern Age," in K. Solga (ed.), *A Cultural History of Theatre in the Modern Age*, 75–94, London: Bloomsbury.

Stanislavsky, K. (2008), *An Actor's Work*, trans. J. Benedetti, London: Routledge.

Taylor, D. (1997), *Disappearing Acts: Spectacles of Gender and Nationalism in Argentina's "Dirty War,"* Durham, NC: Duke University Press.

Tompkins, J. (2006), *Unsettling Space: Contestations in Contemporary Australian Theatre*, Basingstoke: Palgrave Macmillan.

Tompkins, J. (2012), "The 'Place' and Practice of Site-Specific Theatre and Performance," in A. Birch and J. Tompkins (eds.), *Performing Site-Specific Theatre: Politics, Place, Practice*, 1–21, Basingstoke: Palgrave Macmillan.

Tompkins, J. (2014), *Theatre's Heterotopias: Performance and the Cultural Politics of Space*, Basingstoke and New York: Palgrave Macmillan.

Turner, H. (2006), *The English Renaissance Stage: Geometry, Poetics, and the Practical Spatial Arts, 1580–1630*, Oxford: Oxford University Press.

The Unknown Island (2017), Dir. E. McDougall, Gate Theatre, London.

"Visual Story for the Relaxed Performance of *Kiinalik: These Sharp Tools*" (2018), *Buddies in Bad Times Theatre*, March 2. http://buddiesinbadtimes.com/wp-content/uploads/Visual-Story-Kiinalik-These-Sharp-Tools.pdf.

Vizenor, G. (1999), *Manifest Manners: Narratives on Postindian Survivance*, Lincoln, NE: University of Nebraska Press.

Whybrow, N. (2010), *Performance and the Contemporary City: An Interdisciplinary Reader*, Basingstoke: Palgrave Macmillan.

Wiles, D. ([2003] 2007), *A Short History of Western Performance Space*, Cambridge: Cambridge University Press.

Williams, K. (2006), "Anti-Theatricality and the Limits of Naturalism," in A. Ackerman and M. Puchner (eds.), *Against Theatre: Creative Destructions on the Modernist Stage*, 95–112, New York: Palgrave Macmillan.

Wolfe, P. (2006), "Settler Colonialism and the Elimination of the Native," *Journal of Genocide Research*, 8 (4): 387–409.

FURTHER READING

If you would like to explore further, here are some key texts to help you make a start. Some readings have been referenced in this book, while others are new. All are grouped according to core disciplinary areas discussed in sections one and three.

The "Spatial Turn" in Theatre and Performance Studies

Bennett, S. and M. Polito, eds. (2014), *Performing Environments: Site-Specificity in Medieval and Early Modern English Drama*, Basingstoke: Palgrave.

Carlson, M. (1989), *Places of Performance: The Semiotics of Theatre Architecture*, Ithaca, NY: Cornell University Press.

Fuchs, E. and U. Chaudhuri, eds. (2002), *Land/Scape/Theater*, Ann Arbor, MI: University of Michigan Press.

Hopkins, D. J., S. Orr, and K. Solga, eds. (2009), *Performance and the City*, London and Basingstoke: Palgrave MacMillan.

McAuley, G. (1999), *Space in Performance: Making Meaning in the Theatre*, Ann Arbor, MI: University of Michigan Press.

McKinnie, M. (2007), *Space and the Geographies of Theatre*, Toronto: Playwrights Canada Press.

Tompkins, J. (2014), *Theatre's Heterotopias*, London and Basingstoke: Palgrave MacMillan.

The "Social Turn" in Human Geography

Bachelard, G. ([1958] 1994), *The Poetics of Space*, rev. ed., Boston, MA: Beacon Press.

De Certeau, M. (1984), *The Practice of Everyday Life*, trans. S. Rendall, Berkeley, CA: University of California Press.

Foucault, M. ([1967] 1986), "Of Other Spaces: Utopias and Heterotopias," trans. Jay Miskowiec, *Diacritics*, 16 (1): 22–7.

Hanssen, B., ed. (2006), *Walter Benjamin and the Arcades Project*, London: Bloomsbury.
Hetherington, K. (1997), *The Badlands of Modernity: Heterotopia and Social Ordering*, London: Routledge.
Massey, D. (2005), *For Space*, London: Sage.
Merrifield, A. (2006), *Henri Lefebvre: A Critical Introduction*, London: Routledge.

Embodied Space and the Environmental Turn in Theatre Studies and Design Theory

Aronson, A. (2018), *The History and Theory of Environmental Scenography*, 2nd ed., London: Methuen Drama.
Garner, S. (1994), *Bodied Spaces: Phenomenology and Performance in Contemporary Drama*, Ithaca, NY: Cornell University Press.
Levin, L. (2014), *Performing Ground: Space, Camouflage and the Art of Blending In*, Basingstoke: Palgrave Macmillan.
Lotker, S., and R. Gough, eds. (2013), "On Scenography," *Performance Research*, 18 (3).
Shepherd, S. (2005), *Theatre, Body and Pleasure*, London: Routledge.

Decolonizing Theatrical Space

Knowles, R. and Y. Nolan, eds. (2016), *Performing Indigeneity*, Toronto: Playwrights Canada Press.
Lowman, E. B. and A. J. Barker (2015), *Settler: Identity and Colonialism in 21st Century Canada*, Winnipeg: Fernwood Publishing.
Nolan, Y. (2015), *Medicine Shows: Indigenous Performance Culture*, Toronto: Playwrights Canada Press.
Robinson, D. (2015), "Reconciling Relations," *Canadian Theatre Review*, 161: 64–73.
Tompkins, J. (2006), *Unsettling Space: Contestations in Contemporary Australian Theatre*, Basingstoke: Palgrave MacMillan.

INDEX